Heavenly Realm Publishing
Houston, Texas

Position Your *Faith* for Great *Success*

WORK BOOK

VOLUME 1

EACH CHAPTER OFFERS A POWERFUL *7 DAY SERIES OF STUDY AND FAST* TO PUSH YOU TOWARDS YOUR PURPOSE IN LIFE

Stephanie Franklin

Unless otherwise indicated, all scriptures quotations
in this book are from the Holy Bible King James Version, Amplified, and NIV version.

Copyright © 2010 *by,* Stephanie Franklin.
All rights reserved.

Copyright © 2010 Position Your Faith for Great Success *Workbook.*
Volume 1. *By,* Stephanie Franklin
All rights reserved.

Cover Illustration and Design © 2010, Stephanie Franklin,
Heavenly Realm Publishing.
All rights reserved.

ISBN—13:   978-0-9825589-5-9

Library of Congress Control Number: 2010929341

This book is printed on acid free paper.

Printed in the United States of America

No part of this book may be reproduced, stored in a retrieval system, or transmitted by any means, electronic, mechanical, photocopying, recording, or otherwise, without written permission from the author.

Published By:
Heavenly Realm Publishing
505 N. Sam Houston Pkwy. E., Suite 670, Houston, Texas 77060,
toll free 1-877-599-3237.

Enjoy your life where you are and do not worry about your tomorrow.
God will take care of your tomorrow.

~Stephanie Franklin~

Purchase the book, "Position Your Faith for Great Success". It will be challenging to complete this workbook successfully if you do not, or have not purchased the book first. I encourage you to be committed and to dedicate each day until you are completely done with this workbook. It will challenge you to study your bible, understand how to fast and how to move God in your circumstances. What moves God? You will find out by reading, writing, and studying the book and workbook.

More Books by Stephanie:

When Ramona Got Her Groove Back from God
My Song of Solomon
My Song of Solomon *Prayer Journal*
Position Your Faith for Great Success *(Book)*

Welcome To: "Position Your Faith for Great Success *Workbook*". Inside you will find questions over the chapters in the book: "Position Your Faith for Great Success", a 7-day series of study, fast, bible quizzes, daily morning & evening bible reading, daily promises, and day by day grace confession of faith.

I speak God's favor and determination as you complete the challenge this workbook has. I know you can pull it off. As you work independently on this workbook you may also work on it with a bible study group, a study group, in a book club meeting, social gathering, a workshop, a seminar; it can also be used in a church workshop, seminar, or may also be used as a bible study lesson. Hope you have read the book first you'll need it to complete this workbook successfully.

Position Your *Faith* for Great *Success*

WORK BOOK

VOLUME 1

CONTENTS

Before you start the workbook, Position Your Faith for Great Success

Introduction.......The Welcome............................	
Preface......Faith without Works is Dead..............	1
Day by Day Grace Prayer Confession of Faith...........	5

FAITH SESSION 1	11
FAITH SESSION 2	91
FAITH SESSION 3	173
FAITH SESSION 4	247

7-DAY SERIES OF STUDY & FAST	305
DAILY MORNING & EVENING BIBLE READING	315

| QUESTIONS & ANSWERS OF SUCCESS | 333 |

| BIBLE QUIZZES | 337 |

| DAILY PROMISES | 353 |

INTRODUCTION.....*The Welcome*

Welcome to, Position Your Faith for Great Success *Workbook*. You are about to experience a powerful life changing experience of your life. This workbook is about to keep you on the edge of your seat and on your toes. Have you ever had something to challenge you to get better? At first it was quit difficult to receive, understand, or comprehend, but as you did not give up, you kept on working at it or working on it, you began and receive it, understand it, and comprehend it. There are times in our lives when we need a challenge in order to get us to the next level in life. God is responsible for the type of challenges that you may be facing right now if you are following Him. He brings these challenges because He is ready for you to move to your next level. Remember in the Book, "Position Your Faith for Great Success"? I talked about your purpose is like going up your ladder of life and you never know when God is ready for you to take your next step? Well it's the same here, as you begin working, reading, and writing in this workbook, you may work individually or with a group of all sorts as I stated before. It's more fun when working in groups, although, you will still get the same experience as you work alone.

PREFACE

Faith without Works is Dead…..

Positioning your faith for great success is something that has to be put into action daily. For without faith it is impossible to please God. *[James 2:14-26]* God requires that you have faith in order to accomplish any goal or career that you set out to fulfill. It's proven in His word. You must show action—action is a verb, and a verb shows action. What this means is that you must get up from where you are and get out there and **DO** what ever it takes to make your dreams come true. You may be asking these questions, "How do I do this? It's been over 15-20 years since I've been back in school I can't possibly go back and get my high school diploma or my college degree? I'm not sure they will hire me so I'll just keep waiting at my house for my change to come. I've been told all of my life that I wasn't going to be anything so why should I have high hopes for a dream to become anybody now and it all be shattered right before my eyes? My dad wasn't there for me, my mom wasn't there either, so what's the use? Why believe in me, nobody has ever believed in me before? Why start now?" You may be speaking these things right now, whether you are speaking them verbally, or speaking them within yourself, you are still guilty of faith without works. Do not allow your past, or the fact that your mom, dad, family, or friends wasn't there to hinder you from fulfilling your dream or going after the career that you know you can excel in. Nobody can fulfill your dream or your purpose but you; and they certainly can't do it for you. You have to do it yourself. Nobody has the power to stop your dream or purpose from coming to past, unless you give them power over you to stop it. Remember as you read, write, study, and work in this Workbook, ask God to increase your faith to believe for the great success that you are promised to have through Jesus Christ and you will have it; He's waiting to give it to you.

In order to obtain great knowledge you have to first realize that your ideas are important no matter how hard they may seem to come to past or to fulfill. This is why it is important to listen to the giver. The giver is the person or person's who is doing the giving. They may give you information or knowledge in the form of words or in the form of action. While you are listening, learning, and receiving from the giver, this may be a man, a woman, a child, or even a group of people. I have found that some people learn by listening, while others learn by visual. The listeners have to listen to the knowledge that is being given in order to know what is being taught; and to know what to do with the information that is being taught, if this makes sense. For example, let's say that I am the giver. I am teaching you how to get out and get a job while obtaining great success in doing this. This works both in the spiritual and in the physical, and for the learner as well as the visual learner.

First

THIS IS THE SPIRITUAL:
- Look in the bible in the concordance and find the words, faith or promise or any other scriptures that you may know already that has to do with success. Your scripture can even come from a story from the bible.
- Take those scriptures and write them down and tape them on your mirror—a place that you normally look at daily.

THIS IS THE PHYSICAL:
- Get up, wash your face, and get your clothes on.

Second

THIS IS THE SPIRITUAL:
- Confess your scriptures constantly. Trust me this is faith and not a religious act. God moves on faith and when you stand on His word. He said in His word to make your petitions made known to Him. And He will also give you the desires of your heart. *[Psalms 37:4, Psalms 20:5, 1 John 5:15]*

THIS IS THE PHYSICAL:
- Go to the grocery store and get a FREE newspaper and see what jobs are available.
- When you find one or some, write them down with a cheerful and positive attitude.

Third

THIS IS THE SPIRITUAL:

- Stand on those scriptures you wrote down by reading confessing and believing that they are true and that God's word does not lie.

THIS IS THE PHYSICAL:

- Go to the mall or to the job you read in the newspaper and put in applications at the stores or the job that is hiring.

Fourth

THIS IS THE SPIRITUAL & THE PHYSICAL:

- Wait on God to move, while repeating the list over and over each day until God moves for you. It normally doesn't take very long if you believe and do not speak negative words against it, yourself, or your situation. This brings a set back. So be very careful what you speak out of your mouth. Speak nothing but positive words of faith like, "I know I'm going to get that job." "I have no doubts that God is going to keep His word and bless me today with a job." And the list goes on.

By doing these steps, you are showing **FAITH WITH WORKS** and you will be one step closer to great success. What is great success in these steps? Great success is you having a chance to get a job that you did not have before, go to work everyday that you did not have before, start in the position that you never had before, be on time, and do what your boss tells you to do. By doing this you will work your way up in the company. You have a great chance to become a manager or a supervisor on even move up to the vice president's position. This is how you obtain great success. Make sense? Hope so. Again, this works for the listener and for the visual learner.

DAY BY DAY GRACE
PRAYER CONFESSION OF FAITH

ADD YOUR OWN CONFESSION OF FAITH TO WHAT GOD HAS PROMISED YOU WITH THESE SCRIPTURES

*(What is a confession of faith? A confession of faith is when you verbally speak in to existence something that you are **believing** God for in faith. As you speak this, you **believe** by faith that God will hear your prayer confession and move for you.)*

Put these prayer confessions into action daily and watch God move……

| MONDAY | 1 CHRONICLES 17: 23, 25-27 |

| TUESDAY | ROMANS 4: 13-22 |

Position Your Faith for Great Success Workbook

| **WEDNESDAY** | **ROMANS 5: 2-4** |

| **THURSDAY** | **ROMANS 10:17** |

| **FRIDAY** | **ACTS 1:4** |

Stephanie Franklin

SATURDAY — **ACTS 2:39**

SUNDAY — **2 CORINTHIANS 1:20, NUMBERS 23:20**

As I stated earlier that it will be very difficult to complete this workbook without first purchasing and reading my book that goes with it called, "Position Your Faith For Great Success". There again, I challenge you to read my book and you will find the answers to the discussion questions in each faith session. Also be ready to tackle the bible quizzes, the daily morning and evening bible readings, stand on daily promises, and day by day grace confession of faith. I speak God's favor for you, I know you can do it!

FAITH SESSION 1

> **Let's pray before you begin.**
>
> Lord grant _____ the ability and the knowledge to complete this workbook. I thank You that _____ will never be the same after completing and reading this workbook. In Jesus Name, Amen.

FAITH SESSION 1

Birthing Your Purpose from Your Pain

This chapter deals with the most profound subject of the book. It deals with the _____ and the _____. It is important that you get delivered from your _____ in order to go to the next level of faith in your life. It will be hard to go forth in the fullness of God until you are totally free from your _____. I have learned in my years of ministry that God cannot completely use you until you have totally released your _____. Please do not get me wrong, you can still operate in your ministry or be used by God, but if you want to be used to the fullness, you must get free from your _____.

Answer the following questions from the book.

FAITH SESSION 1—Questions from the book.

Questions	DAY BY DAY GRACE CONFESSION OF FAITH
What is the key subject in Chapter One? After you write your answer below, discuss it with someone or in a group.	My life is headed in a direction of success. I have the choice to pull back, or the choice to press forward. I will choose _____
Can you tell me where and what page can you find this sentence? "Your purpose is what you were sent to the earth to do…."	
What was the number one encouragement that I told you in this chapter?	

Why were these scriptures used in this chapter? Isaiah 44:2, Jeremiah 1:5, and Jeremiah 29:11. _____ _____ How do you win a person to Christ? _____ _____ _____ What was the story that I shared and how has it helped you in your own life? _____ _____ _____	**DAY BY DAY GRACE CONFESSION OF FAITH** If no one believes in me I will still _____ _____ _____ _____ _____ _____ _____

The more you go through, the greater the anointing. I'm not saying to go and steal a car and go to prison for 10 years and this will prove that you went through for the anointing nor is the anointing on your life great. No, that's not nearly what I am saying. You cannot do wrong and say that that was God's doing; that certainly has nothing to do with the anointing. That has everything to do with bad choices. Bad choices will keep you from fulfilling God's best in your life. But what I am saying is if you're being persecuted for living for God. When people hate you for nothing and all you're trying to do is live for God, stay faithful, and do a work for Him, then this is for you. This is going through for the anointing. The bible teaches us that we will be persecuted because Jesus was. This is why it says blessed are you who are persecuted for righteousness. *[Matthew 5:10]* So don't give up because you're being persecuted, be encouraged. Also, allow God to use you to the fullest by releasing your _____ and move forward so that you can receive all that God has for you.

HOW DO I GET FREE FROM THE PAIN OF MY PAST?

1. **You must first forgive the one who has hurt you.** I realize this is hard but it must be done. Put yourself in the position of the one who has done the hurting. I'm sure you've hurt someone in your life time and wanted so badly for them to forgive you? Right? Well it works the same here. I know it's a tough pill to swallow when you're on

the receiving end like I mentioned earlier. The bible says that we must forgive if we want to be forgiven. *[Luke 6:37]*

2. **You must release them.** You must release the person or persons who have hurt you. I realize it's hard because I've been there. I had to release my father, I had to release some church folks, I had to release some so called friends, and so on throughout my life time; this was the only way that I could move on and receive all that God had for me. I could not successfully walk in the fullness with peace of mind until they were released from my heart, mind, spirit, and soul. This is why I shared the testimony in my book to help you and others see that you're not alone; and the fact that you can come out of it and move on with your life. You must forgive and release those who have hurt you because if you look at it, they're gone on with their lives and have moved on enjoying themselves while you're still living in the past still mad, hurt, angry, full of hatred wishing they would die or hurt or harm would come to them or wishing the same thing they did to you would happen to them. This is not the will of God for you and for your life. God wants you at peace. He wants you to love your enemies and pray for them and bless them and allow God to take care of them. It's not up to us to take vengeance, only God can take vengeance, and trust me, He does it very well. God is love and He specializes in unity, love, and restoration He doesn't specialize in hurting people.

3. **You must move on with your life.** The last thing I want to say is, do not be jealous of the one who has hurt you if it appears that they are prospering and are blessed and you're going through, the bible says that their day will come and you do not have to be jealous or wish bad against them. Got it? I sure hope so. I whole heartedly understand your hurt and your pain, but you must release it/them and move on with your life. This is my prayer for you. You'll feel so much better when you do. How do you know that you're free, is when someone says their name around you and anger does not build up on the inside of you, or thoughts of evil or hatred does not clutter your mind against them. That's when you know you're free and have moved on with your life. This topic is good for group discussion, I encourage this. I have found that sometimes getting with a group that is Spirit filled, who you can trust and open up too, will help towards your freedom and make your deliverance lighter, easier, and love filled.

Take the points that I just gave you and discuss them in a group. This is a time to talk about your own personal experiences.

TAKE YOUR NOTES

Stephanie Franklin

> **Write down what you have received from the chapter and how it applies to your own life. How have your eyes been open? What areas will you change? What area(s) of success in your life will this benefit? Share your story by writing it below.**

Stephanie Franklin

Stephanie Franklin

FAITH SESSION 1

Hell Faith to Heaven Faith

Having faith is not always easy to do. In fact, it's very hard when you're going through and can't see how God is going to get you out of that particular situation. In the chapter Hell Faith to Heaven Faith, one thing you must remember is that God is good and there is no one who can do better than Him. God is what makes the earth turn around. He is what supplies the earth with plants and herbs for seed and nutrition. God is what keeps the roaring seas back from swallowing us up. God is everything. For more in depth reading, resort back to the book. GOD GETS ALL OF THE GLORY. In the book I discuss this in detail. You must know that all of your strength, power, healing, deliverance, favor, resources, business deals, stock, pension plans, career choices, career success, high school diploma, college degree, brand new homes, relationships, children getting saved, marriages—husbands and wives turning to God, and more. All of these facts must be centered around God, and God alone. God may have allowed you to lead in these types of positions, but you must always remember that He does not need you, you need Him and you can't lead or operate in these positions by yourself. It is God Who sets you on top, and it is Him Who can tare you down. If you think that you are the king and God can't tell you anything, this is what I call, Hell faith. But when you humble yourself, always know that you are nothing without God, and that it is Him who helps you lead and to be led, this is Heaven Faith. And if you are operating in the Hell faith mentality, you can repent, ask God to forgive you, and turn your faith to Heaven faith.

Position Your Faith for Great Success Workbook

Answer the following questions from the book.

FAITH SESSION 1—Questions from the book.

What is meant by Hell Faith to Heaven Faith?
If you do not believe in God is this Hell Faith or Heaven Faith? Why? Provide page number to back your answer up.
What does the scripture Galatians 6:14 say in the chapter? How is it being used? How can this be applied to your life?

DAY BY DAY GRACE CONFESSION OF FAITH

My life is headed in a direction of success. I have the choice to pull back, or the choice to press forward. I will choose _____

What am I talking about concerning this sentence? *"This is what the devil believes..."* Elaborate using the extra space provided.
Can God lie? Find the answer in the chapter.
How does this chapter relate to your own life? Use the extra writing space below for addition space to answer.

DAY BY DAY GRACE CONFESSION OF FAITH

If no one believes in me I will still _____

Take the information from the session and discuss them with another person or in a group. You and each one in the group take a piece of paper and fold it in half, on the left side write down the areas you have not been trusting in God. And on the right side write down how you plan to trust God in those areas. Discuss what you have written.

TAKE YOUR NOTES

Stephanie Franklin

> **Write down what you have received from the chapter and how it applies to your own life. How have your eyes been open? What areas will you change? What area(s) of success in your life will this benefit? Share your story by writing it below.**

Stephanie Franklin

Stephanie Franklin

FAITH SESSION 1

Faith as Easy as Saying 1, 2, 3

Most people think faith as easy as saying 1, 2, 3 is not as simple as it is to say it. Faith really is that simple. I have to remind myself that this is really true. We make faith seem too hard especially when we pray and nothing happens. We're quick to say that saying doesn't work. One thing you have to remember is, just because your prayers haven't been answered when you wanted them too, doesn't mean that God has not made plans to answer them. It's just in His time and in His season. Many times it's a test just to see if you're going to be patient and allow God to be God. You must trust Him in all of your ways. In His word He tells you in *[Proverbs 3:5-6]* to put our trust in the Lord with ALL of your heart, and lean not to your own understanding, but in ALL your ways <u>acknowledge Him</u> and <u>He will direct your path</u>. This scripture is very important to your everyday routine. In fact, in your confession you should add this scripture in it. To trust God in all your ways no matter what comes your way. I know by experience it's not easy, especially when the enemy is right in your face trying to put you on blast and waiting to see if you're going to put Him on blast and embarrass yourself and the God in you. It's not easy being a "Christian" everyday. In fact I believe it's more of a challenge to be a Christian than not. The devil comes at you in all kinds of directions that if you're not rooted and grounded and have a safe Haven to turn too, you would go flat crazy. I have learned that if the devil doesn't come at you with his tricks and schemes, you're not a threat. But God will always provide a way for you to escape his evil plans, tricks, and schemes. *[1 Corinthians 10:13]* This is what makes it easy because God will always cover, bless, and protect you.

I'm not contradicting myself when I say that faith is as easy as saying 1, 2, 3. I'm basing this from God's word. He says in *[Matthew 21:22]* that what ever you ask in prayer, believing, you shall receive. That is faith as easy as saying 1, 2, 3.

How do I do this faith as easy as 1, 2, 3 thing?

1. Go to your pantry or where ever you store your food.
2. Pull out a box or a product that you like with cooking instructions on it.
3. Read the instructions and follow exactly what those instructions tell you to do.

4. After you do exactly what it tells you to do, come back to the workbook and write down the outcome of you doing what the instructions told you to do.

BREAK TO DO EXERCISE*********************************

If you are reading this sentence, I'm assuming that you have already done the exercise? Well, I sure hope so because if you can see the benefit and better understanding in this, it will help you understand how easy faith is. Read how I have explained this exercise more in depth below.

Share on the lines below and/or in a group what you received and learned from this exercise?

_____
_____
_____
_____
_____
_____
_____
_____

Now that you have shared, allow me to explain why I told you to do this exercise. This is the answer to why I said faith is as easy as 1, 2, 3. If you just follow what God says in the bible, giving you what He has promised *[Romans 4:20-21]*, this is the answered ingredient to all of your prayers, problems, dilemmas, situations, getting free from struggles, life itself, etc. I can say for myself, when I follow God's plan—His word, write out scriptures, stand on them daily, go on a fast, my prayers are always answered right away. But when I don't, they don't. Most of the time night can't come quick enough because God has already answered my prayers. To the flesh, it would seem like a lot of work and the flesh struggles with that and does not want you to do that, but this is the answer to successfully get what you want, need, and desire if you follow the instructions.

Now let's answer the questions from the book.

Stephanie Franklin

Answer the following questions from the book.

FAITH SESSION 1—Questions from the book.

What is the rod that God is talking about in this chapter?	**DAY BY DAY GRACE CONFESSION OF FAITH** I will get through my attacks. I will not give up because
Finish this sentence: "As quick as it takes us to say, 1, 2, 3…" After you finish it, how does it apply to your own life?	
Who is David having the fight with in this chapter? How does he defeat him?	

What is meant by, "it will not fail"?	**DAY BY DAY GRACE CONFESSION OF FAITH** If no one believes in me I will still
What is meant about, "crazy faith"?	
How does this chapter relate to your own life? Use the extra writing space below for additional space to answer.	

35

> Take the information from the session and discuss them in a group. Group discussion: Talk and write down all of the giants in your life and how you have or plan to overcome them. They may be a person, people, family, husband or wife, rebellious children, bills, finances, sickness in your body.

TAKE YOUR NOTES

Stephanie Franklin

Write down what you have received from the chapter and how it applies to your own life. How have your eyes been open? What areas will you change? What area(s) of success in your life will this benefit? Share your story by writing it below.

Stephanie Franklin

Stephanie Franklin

FAITH SESSION 1

Prosperity Come to me Right Now!

The bible says that money answers all things. *[Ecclesiastes 10:19]* So if it answers all things, this simply means that it's important to have it. This also means that God wants us to have it. God wants you to have exceedingly abundantly, above all that you could ask or think, but it's according to the power that works in you. *[Ephesians 3:20]* God has given us power to obtain wealth. Just like Heaven is filled with Heavenly riches and wealth, this earth is filled with abundance of riches and wealth. It is God's greatest desire that we are wealthy and well taken care of. I've never known a poor leader that belonged to the Lord. They were all well taken care of. Tests and trials may have come their way, but God kept His word; and this is what He wants to do for you. Call in your wealth, call in your riches, **"Prosperity come to me right now!"**

Steps to Prosperity coming to you right now:

1. Write out the areas where you are in the red (where you are financially in dept).
2. Write down what you have in your bank account.
3. Look in the bible and find scriptures on prosperity and promise, and God meeting your needs.
4. Every check you get, put back $10-20 dollars or higher in a savings or private place, save it about four to six months. Then take what you've saved up and pay a bill that is easiest to pay. Please do not try to pay the bills that are extremely too high unless you come into abundance of wealth. Take the small and work your way up. This is how you can clean up your credit as well. Do not be unreasonable and try to pay a school loan that's $50,000 or higher and you only make a pay check of $200 a week. Pay what is the easiest and work your way up. Make sense? Share with others.

Write down how much you've saved, write down what bills you've paid on or out? Now write down how they have helped you. Did the steps I gave you work?

Position Your Faith for Great Success Workbook

_____
_____
_____
_____
_____
_____
_____

Now let's answer the questions from the book.

Answer the following questions from the book.

FAITH SESSION 1—Questions from the book.

What is meant by "Prosperity Come to me Right Now"?	**DAY BY DAY GRACE CONFESSION OF FAITH**
What is this sentence talking about? "Please do not miss your time waiting on God to make the first move."	God's word says this about my finances
What is meant by this sentence? "When God is ready to take you to the next level do you have a choice?"	

Pg. 119. Do you believe this is your appointed year by this sentence from the chapter? "I believe this is the year and the season for the saints to receive everything that God has promised." Elaborate on your answer.	**DAY BY DAY GRACE CONFESSION OF FAITH** If no one believes in me I will still
What is this phrase talking about? "It's yours for the asking and the taking?	
What is meant by this? "But in the end when his so called friends found out that it was all God who orchestrated the entire test..."	

Take the information from the session and discuss them in a group. Group discussion: Talk about what you have written down concerning how much you have saved, what bills you've paid on or out, how you wrote them down, and how they have helped you. Talk about the steps.

TAKE YOUR NOTES

Stephanie Franklin

Write down what you have received from the chapter and how it applies to your own life. How have your eyes been open? What areas will you change? What area(s) of success in your life will this benefit? Share your story by writing it below.

Position Your Faith for Great Success Workbook

Stephanie Franklin

Position Your Faith for Great Success Workbook

Stephanie Franklin

Stephanie Franklin

Stephanie Franklin

FAITH SESSION 1

Don't Panic, it's Only a Test

Don't Panic, It's Only a Test. This chapter is a sensitive subject for most people because when catastrophe comes in our lives, fear and panic is the first reaction. As trials and tribulations come your way, you think that God is punishing you, but He's not. It's only a test that comes to make you strong. They bring patience and endurance so that God's glory shall be revealed in you.

Tests come in all kinds of ways. You do not choose how you want to be tested. In fact, you never know when you're going to be tested, where you're going to be tested, and who is going to be used to test you. This is why it is good to be spiritually girded up so when the fiery darts come, you're covered with the whole armour of God. Look at the example below. This is how you should be girded up <u>spiritually</u>. <u>PLEASE DO NOT</u> do this physically; it's not necessary to go that far. Smiling… But this is necessary spiritually because the man is showing the strength in Jesus you should have with all of the spiritual armours. Take a look and study it. Do you understand the importance?

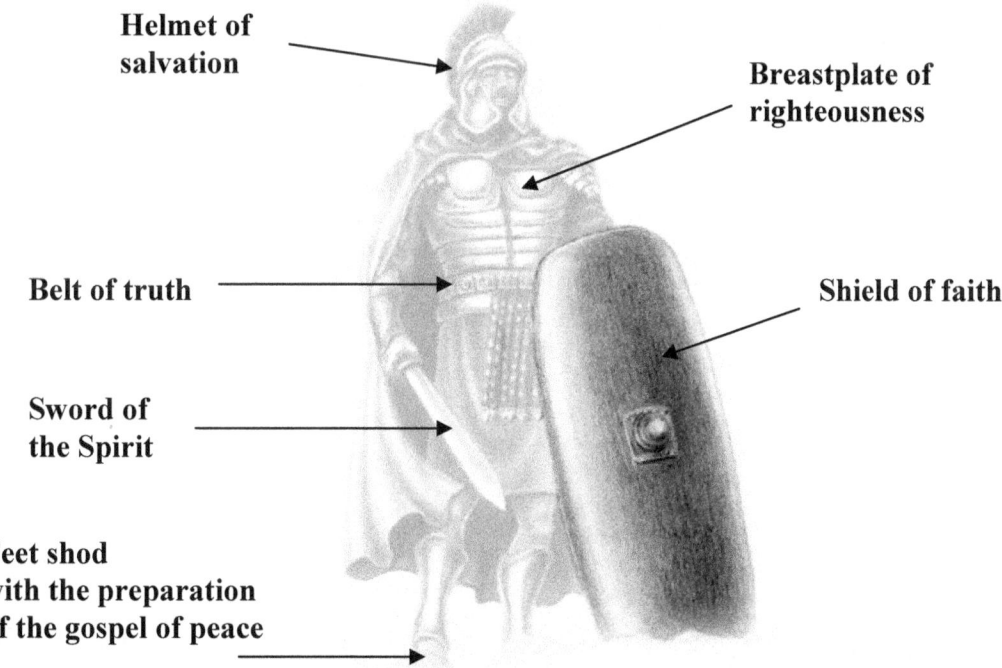

- **Helmet of salvation**
- **Breastplate of righteousness**
- **Belt of truth**
- **Shield of faith**
- **Sword of the Spirit**
- **Feet shod with the preparation of the gospel of peace**

As you study the roman soldier that is fully equipped for battle, you can see this is a great example of how you as a Christian, a child of God must be equipped for battle when the devil tries to come and steal what is rightfully yours—your peace, your joy, your mind, your job, your family, your marriage, attacking your memory while taking a test at school, your dream, your accomplishments, your success, your purpose, your promise, and the business that God has promised you. You have got to be ready at all times. These are the areas where the devil likes to attack and he will try to steal what ever he can if you are not covered and you do not have your whole armour of God on daily. It says in **[Ephesians 6:11-18]** *-[16] Put on the whole armour of God, that ye may be able to stand against the wiles of the devil. [17] And take the helmet of salvation, and the sword of the Spirit, which is the word of God: [18] Praying always with all prayer and supplication in the Spirit, and watching thereunto with all perseverance and supplication for all saints;* This is the word of God and in order to pass any test, you must have your armour on daily. You must be equipped and ready to conquer anything that may come your way daily. Don't get me wrong, it takes work for all of us, but I'm a strong believer that if we all say, pray, and believe the day by day prayer confession of faith in this workbook and the prayer confession of faith for each day of the week in the "Position Your Faith for Great Success" Book every morning before we leave our homes, pray that God will cancel every assignment that the enemy will try to send against you each day, live according to God's word, trust Him for a good day of success, treat everybody right with love and unity, this will completely teach you how to fight and turn your life a round. You will literally have great success in your life, business, home, on your job, in school, in your mind, body, spirit, and soul. This will bring victory and the ultimate peace that is so much needed daily. Do you believe this? I sure hope so.

Let's go to the chapter, "Don't Panic, It's Only a Test" in the book. I want to test you to see if you have read and to see if it has helped you. Are you ready? Ok, here we go.

Stephanie Franklin

Answer the following questions from the book.

FAITH SESSION 1—Questions from the book.

What is meant by, "You see my glory, but you don't know my story."? Use what is said in the chapter, not your testimony.

How are the words, "church hurt" being used in this chapter? Explain.

Expound on this statement in the chapter: "If we never have any enemies, we will never be challenged; and therefore we would get comfortable, and never go higher; therefore we would never fulfill the purpose that God has for us to fulfill."

DAY BY DAY GRACE CONFESSION OF FAITH

The devil will not attack me because

From this statement, "HE DID NOT PANIC, BECAUSE HE KNEW THAT IT WAS ONLY A TEST." Who are they talking about?

Name the scripture that this statement is talking about. "He does not do it through unbelief, but is fully persuaded that what ever He promised you, He is more than able to perform it.

What was the covenant that God made with Abraham in this chapter? And what type of relationship did they have?

DAY BY DAY GRACE CONFESSION OF FAITH

The devil will not attack me because

> Take the information from the session and discuss them in a group. Group discussion: Talk about a time when you were tested and the enemy was right in your face. Tell the group how you handled it negatively or positively. If your response was negative, talk about how you plan to pass the next test that may come your way.

TAKE YOUR NOTES

Stephanie Franklin

Write down what you have received from the chapter and how it applies to your own life. How have your eyes been open? What areas will you change? What area(s) of success in your life will this benefit? Share your story by writing it below.

Position Your Faith for Great Success Workbook

Stephanie Franklin

Position Your Faith for Great Success Workbook

Stephanie Franklin

Position Your Faith for Great Success Workbook

Stephanie Franklin

Stephanie Franklin

Position Your Faith for Great Success Workbook

FAITH SESSION 1

It's a Set Up

The chapter, "It's a Set Up" is based on the fact that you're going through a rough time and it seems as if God isn't with you, but I want you to know that He is. Your success is not based on where you been, it's based on where you are going. You may have been through terrible times in your life and you may have been told that you're not going to make it, but rest assure you will.

Let's go to the chapter and see if you can remember what it says about you being set up for great success and not for failure.

Answer the following questions from the book.

FAITH SESSION 1—Questions from the book.

Questions	DAY BY DAY GRACE CONFESSION OF FAITH
Can you tell me where this sentence is in this chapter? "Giving up cannot be in your vocabulary."	My future success is not defined by my past failures because
How is Matthew 26:36-42 being used in this chapter? What are your thoughts on it?	
What is the revelation to this sentence? "…One of those adhesives I use is called: "Elmer's Glue-All". It is a Multi-PURPOSE GLUE…"	

Finish this sentence from the chapter, "Just as this type of glue is intended for the use of adhesively bonding something together..."

_____
_____
_____

True or False. God is strictly intended to supply everything you stand in need of according to the purpose in which He has already set for you to accomplish.

_____
_____
_____

How is Jeremiah 29:11 being used in the chapter? Please answer according to what is written in the chapter.

_____
_____
_____
_____

DAY BY DAY GRACE CONFESSION OF FAITH

My future success is not defined by my past failures because

_____
_____
_____
_____
_____
_____
_____

Take the information from the session and discuss them in a group. Group discussion: Take a time when you were in a position where it seemed as if you were set up for failure or embarrassment and you felt as if God was no where to be found. What did you do? How did you handle it?

Stephanie Franklin

TAKE YOUR NOTES

Position Your Faith for Great Success Workbook

Stephanie Franklin

Write down what you have received from the chapter and how it applies to your own life. How have your eyes been open? What areas will you change? What area(s) of success in your life will this benefit? Share your story by writing it below.

Stephanie Franklin

Stephanie Franklin

Position Your Faith for Great Success Workbook

Stephanie Franklin

Position Your Faith for Great Success Workbook

FAITH SESSION 2

Let's pray before you begin.

Lord grant _____ the ability and the knowledge to complete this workbook. I thank You that nothing will hinder _____ success while reading and studying this workbook. I thank You that _____ will comprehend and understand what has been written after completing and reading this workbook. In Jesus Name, Amen.

FAITH SESSION 2

Iron Sharpens Iron

The chapter, "Iron Sharpens Iron" is a chapter where God comes to sharpen everything in your life that needs to be sharpened. You cannot have complete, great success until you have certain areas in your life sharpened for success. Most times, those certain areas hurt too bad and some people do not last and give up. This is why I have found for a fact that you cannot make it without the Lord nor without His word to guide you to great success and through great success. I give examples and make real life points to help you, but they will never override God's plan and His word for your life. Iron Sharpens Iron is a great chapter that lines out those areas in your life that may be stopping your success and you may not be aware of it. This chapter shows you, and helps you to repent and renounce those areas and get back on track to have great success in what ever you are believing to have success in. Make sense? I sure hope so. Let's review the chapter with a few questions.

Answer the following questions from the book.

FAITH SESSION 2—Questions from the book.

Questions	DAY BY DAY GRACE CONFESSION OF FAITH
Can you tell me what areas in your life does God want to clean out in this chapter?"	Today I have the victory over.... because...
I mentioned about the refiners fire. What am I talking about and what is your perspective over this subject?	
What is meant by the potter wheel as it is being used in this chapter?	

Position Your Faith for Great Success Workbook

Finish this sentence from the chapter... "They mimic your actions and how you talk....."

How are these words being used in the chapter? "My mind.....my emotions......my attitude...." How does this briefly relate to your own life?

What is the answer to this question from the chapter? "How do I get clean?" How does this apply to your own life?

DAY BY DAY GRACE CONFESSION OF FAITH

Today I have the victory over.... because...

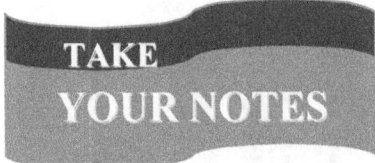

Take the information from the session and discuss them in a group. Group discussion: Share about a time where you or a specific situation in your life that God sharpened in order to get you to the place of success today. Everyone should share even if they have not experienced that place. They can share about a time when they have been sharpened to get to the place they are in right now or to be a better person.

Stephanie Franklin

Position Your Faith for Great Success Workbook

Stephanie Franklin

Write down what you have received from the chapter and how it applies to your own life. How have your eyes been open? What areas will you change? What area(s) of success in your life will this benefit? Share your story by writing it below.

Stephanie Franklin

Position Your Faith for Great Success Workbook

FAITH SESSION 2

Two Heads Are Better Than One

God sometimes gives you a vision that requires more than one person to fulfill it. I do not mean that He will give you a vision and allow others to take it over or take it from you; nor do I mean that He will allow others to come and steal and control your vision either. What I mean is that He will send someone or others to help you. They will obey your every command through what God gives you instruction to do. Do you understand this? I sure hope so.

Two heads are better than one because at times one person cannot fulfill the purpose or the ability to have great success alone. Not to make the person who has had others to help you seem weak or lack having enough faith, but when God gives a vision it will always be too large for you to do it alone. You'll have to share because the blessings are much too great. One thing to remember, God will never take from you to give to others and leave you with nothing or not enough or allow them to take or steal your vision from you as I stated before.

Did you read and study the chapter "Two Heads are Better Than One"? Let's see if you can remember.

Position Your Faith for Great Success Workbook

Answer the following questions from the book.

FAITH SESSION 2—Questions from the book.

Why did I make this statement in the chapter? "One thing you have to realize is that you cannot complete your purpose by yourself."

"God will never put two people together and their destinies and plans do not match." What is the next sentence after this one? And what does this mean?

Why does God want you to be happy? What is meant by this sentence? What page is it located on? Apply this to your life.

DAY BY DAY GRACE CONFESSION OF FAITH

Today I have the victory over…. because…

What happens when people jump into relationships too quick?

On page 194, whose plans can you destroy before they manifest? What scripture is based from this?

"When God has assigned certain people to come into your life, be careful that you do not block them out…" Why is this important according to the chapter?

DAY BY DAY GRACE CONFESSION OF FAITH

Today I have the victory over…. because…

Take the information from the session and discuss them in a group. Group discussion: Share about a time when you didn't wait on God in a certain relationship or friendship and moved too fast or did not listen to God's instructions and catastrophe happened. What did you do to come out of it?

TAKE YOUR NOTES

Stephanie Franklin

Position Your Faith for Great Success Workbook

Write down what you have received from the chapter and how it applies to your own life. How have your eyes been open? What areas will you change? What area(s) of success in your life will this benefit? Share your story by writing it below.

Stephanie Franklin

Stephanie Franklin

Stephanie Franklin

FAITH SESSION 2

You Are Special Like the Cedar Tree

This chapter comes from a biblical stand point. It shows how special each person is to God. You may ask, "how does this relate to great success?" Well, if you do not have the confidence to know that you are capable, qualified, and able to have great success, you will not. This is what God is giving you in this chapter. He's letting you know in His word that you can have great success because you are special and nobody can be like you. That means your vision is for you and you alone to fulfill. You are special like that. Negative things may have been said about you in the past, but just know that you are special and very capable of fulfilling your God given talent, vision, and dream. Do you believe that? I sure hope so.

Let's go the chapter question.

Answer the following questions from the book.

FAITH SESSION 2—Questions from the book.

Questions	DAY BY DAY GRACE CONFESSION OF FAITH
Why do people wear masks?	I am special because…
What does Ezekiel 31:1-9 mean to you?	
What happens when you chase after people?	

Position Your Faith for Great Success Workbook

What happens when God begins to bless you according to page 217? _____ _____ _____	**DAY BY DAY GRACE CONFESSION OF FAITH** I am special because...
How does this statement apply to your own life? "He healed you to a greater glory and a greater testimony." *Found on page 217.* _____ _____ _____	_____ _____ _____ _____
Psalms 68:1 says according to this chapter. How is it being used? _____ _____ _____	_____ _____ _____ _____

Take the information from the session and discuss them in a group. Group discussion: Share about a time when you made a person feel special for who they are, or you showed your kindness towards a person which made them feel special.

You may also share a time when you showed your kindness and a person did not feel special or they did not appreciate the kindness you showed. What did you do or how did their actions or attitude make you feel?

Stephanie Franklin

TAKE YOUR NOTES

Stephanie Franklin

Write down what you have received from the chapter and how it applies to your own life. How have your eyes been open? What areas will you change? What area(s) of success in your life will this benefit? Share your story by writing it below.

Stephanie Franklin

Stephanie Franklin

FAITH SESSION 2

Don't Judge A Book by it's Cover

Being judged is not a fun thing especially what people are judging you with is totally wrong. I shared this example in my book about a closed book. You can easily judge what you think that book is about by looking at it from the outside, but when you open it up and read the facts, you'll find that your judgment was all wrong. This is why it is so important to get to know a person by who they are on the inside, rather than by what you see on the outside. Make sense? Sure hope so. Let's go to the chapter, I want to test you over what you've read.

Answer the following questions from the book.

FAITH SESSION 2—Questions from the book.

Questions	DAY BY DAY GRACE CONFESSION OF FAITH
Ever had someone to judge you from what they thought they saw on the outside?" What page is this located on, and how does this apply to you?	I will not be afraid of _____
True or false. Does God want His people to have great success based on page 231-232.	
True or false, God will never give up on you. Explain your answer.	because *(use the bible for reference)* _____

Position Your Faith for Great Success Workbook

Why does God want your future to soar? How does this apply to your own life? _____ _____ _____	**DAY BY DAY GRACE CONFESSION OF FAITH** I will not be afraid of _____ _____ _____ because *(use the bible for reference)* _____ _____ _____
"Do not be afraid of walking and living a life of success." What page is this statement on and how does it apply to your own life? _____ _____ _____	
Take hold of your future! Reposition your faith for greatness for your future! Do you believe this statement? Why? _____ _____ _____	

Take the information from the session and discuss them in a group. Group discussion: Share about a time when someone judge you from the outside and did not get to know you from the inside. Share how it made you feel and how you handled it.

TAKE YOUR NOTES

Stephanie Franklin

Write down what you have received from the chapter and how it applies to your own life. How have your eyes been open? What areas will you change? What area(s) of success in your life will this benefit? Share your story by writing it below.

Stephanie Franklin

Position Your Faith for Great Success Workbook

FAITH SESSION 2

The Potter and the Clay

The Potter and the Clay evolve around one having power over the other. In this case, the Potter has power over the clay because it's trying to make the clump into a master piece. This is what God is trying to do to your life. Allow God to work a work in you. Let's go to the chapter, I want to test you over what you've read.

Answer the following questions from the book.

FAITH SESSION 2—Questions from the book.

Questions	DAY BY DAY GRACE CONFESSION OF FAITH
"...God is trying to make each and every one of us into something beautiful to look at—from the inside out." How does this apply to your own life?	God is delivering me in this/these area/areas _____ _____ _____ He's preparing me for _____ _____
True or false. When you are representing God you are not required to be just like Him. Why or why not?	
Who is the Potter and who is the clay in the chapter?	

Position Your Faith for Great Success Workbook

What is God trying to create in you, He as the Potter and you as the clay?	**DAY BY DAY GRACE CONFESSION OF FAITH** God's plan for my life is
Why do we fight God's purpose and plan for our lives?	
In the first synopsis, what example is used and what is stated in the chart?	

Take the information from the session and discuss them in a group. Group discussion: Share about how God has changed or is changing you into the image of Him. Discuss different areas that He has tested you in and you have past and over came them.

You may also share a time when you might not have past the test. When God is first dealing with you about you, it's normal that you might not get delivered right away. But as you keep allowing Him to work on you, you will eventually change.

TAKE YOUR NOTES

Stephanie Franklin

Position Your Faith for Great Success Workbook

Stephanie Franklin

> **Write down what you have received from the chapter and how it applies to your own life. How have your eyes been open? What areas will you change? What area(s) of success in your life will this benefit? Share your story by writing it below.**

Stephanie Franklin

Stephanie Franklin

Stephanie Franklin

Position Your Faith for Great Success Workbook

FAITH SESSION 2

I Am All That God Says I Am

This chapter is a chapter that is dear to my heart because it is so personal. It's personal because it allows me to feel confident that I am all that God says I am. Remember that you do not have to worry about what people say or what people think because God is for you, and He's more than all them that's against you. You have to know who you are and Whose you are—Who you belong to. God got cho' back….smile… Let's go to the chapter, I want to see if you remember what you have read.

Answer the following questions from the book.

FAITH SESSION 2—Questions from the book.

Questions	DAY BY DAY GRACE CONFESSION OF FAITH
What will make you soon forget that you are special like God says you are?	My latter days will be greater than my past because _____ _____ _____ _____ _____ _____ _____
True or false. Your future may seem very dim, but God will resurrect your future.	
Was Lazarus raised from the dead immediately?	

Position Your Faith for Great Success Workbook

What page is this statement located on? "Your latter days shall be greater than your former days."	**DAY BY DAY GRACE CONFESSION OF FAITH** My latter days will be greater than my past because _____
What page is this statement on? "But when Jesus came into the room, the defeated situation changed into a **resurrection experience** and Lazarus was raised from the dead.	
Is God doubting your situation?	

Take the information from the session and discuss them in a group. Group discussion: Share about how God made you feel special when you were discouraged. He may have spoke it to you, through someone, or you may have heard it on television or by radio. Where ever, share that time.

Share how it made you feel. Recall the situation you were going through and God spoke His word to you.

Stephanie Franklin

TAKE YOUR NOTES

Write down what you have received from the chapter and how it applies to your own life. How has your eyes been open? What areas will you change? What area(s) of success in your life will this benefit? Share your story by writing it below.

Stephanie Franklin

Stephanie Franklin

Stephanie Franklin

FAITH SESSION 3

> **Let's pray before you begin.**
>
> Lord grant _____ the ability and the knowledge to complete this workbook. I thank You that _____ will comprehend and understand what has been written after completing and reading this workbook. I thank You that _____ In Jesus Name, Amen.

FAITH SESSION 3

Can These Dry Bones Resurrect and Live?

When you've done all you can do to stand, just stand. Tests and obstacles may come your way to make you give up, but don't give up. Hang in there. You're only a quitter if you quit. You can never say that you have conquered something successfully if you never tried. So my advice to you is to never give up. Ask yourself this question as I have asked you in the book, "can my dry bones resurrect and live"? Now answer, "Yes, I know they will." You can never give up or give in to life's struggles, problems, and obstacles. Let's see how you do with the questions from the book. Hope you read it, it makes answering the questions easy and possible.

Answer the following questions from the book.

FAITH SESSION 3—Questions from the book.

What is this chapter talking about? *(Must be the exact words from the chapter).*	**DAY BY DAY GRACE CONFESSION OF FAITH** I will live my life again and
"Your circumstances have out weighed what the word of God has told you about God being a promise keeper." What does it talk about next?	
"Can your finances get any better than just making it from pay check to pay check?" What's the answer to this sentence in the chapter?	

Position Your Faith for Great Success Workbook

	DAY BY DAY GRACE CONFESSION OF FAITH
"You've been… following the same ol' people that mean your future no good, you've been doubting yourself and allowing the same ol' people to dictate your life…." What is the Holy Spirit saying after this?	I will live my life again and
True or false. You must rebuke the devil and his tactics to make you quit and abort the promise that God is leading you to, and command your future to be blessed.	
True or false? You have to take hold of your life and command your situation to change by speaking words of faith and using the word of the Lord.	

Take the information from the session and discuss them in a group. Group discussion: Share about how you had or will have to take hold of your life and command your situation to change by speaking words of faith and using the word of God. Also share a time when you had to encourage someone else who may have given up but got their life back because of you and your faith.

TAKE YOUR NOTES

Stephanie Franklin

Write down what you have received from the chapter and how it applies to your own life. How has your eyes been open? What areas will you change? What area(s) of success in your life will this benefit? Share your story by writing it below.

Position Your Faith for Great Success Workbook

Stephanie Franklin

Stephanie Franklin

Stephanie Franklin

FAITH SESSION 3

When My Bones Became Flesh through Faith

Getting your life back from a dead situation is not always an easy thing to do. There's a lot of persevering you must go through. You have to persevere through all of the baggage and all of the residue that your past has caused. You can get through it. This chapter says, "When My Bones Became Flesh through Faith". The key word here is **"WHEN"**. **WHEN** you get back everything that the devil stole from you. **WHEN** you get back everything that all of your haters took from you and situations where you made mistakes yourself and lost things because of it—get ready to get it all back!

Let's see how you've read the chapter.

Answer the following questions from the book.

FAITH SESSION 3—Questions from the book.

Questions	DAY BY DAY GRACE CONFESSION OF FAITH
What was explained in the chapter, "Can These Dry Bones Resurrect and Live?"	My life is made brand new through _____
True or false. You do not have the power to move old, depressing, unimportant things out of your life by simply telling them to move.	
What page is this located on? What is it talking about? "You can get everything that has been stolen from you back."	

Position Your Faith for Great Success Workbook

What page and what scripture is this statement being used as an example? "God can make you new."	**DAY BY DAY GRACE CONFESSION OF FAITH** My life is made brand new through _____ _____ _____ _____ _____ _____ _____
_____ _____	
"You have to literally tell yourself that you can make it and speak God's word…" What is this referring to? What page?	
_____ _____ _____	
How does the statement apply to your own life?	
_____ _____ _____	

Take the information from the session and discuss them in a group. Group discussion: Share about a time in your own life where you had a challenging moment that you did not know how to come out of but later you did. Tell the group how you did it.

Also, look in the book in the 7-Day Series of Study at the end of the chapter. Look on Monday and talk about when you were in your dry land and how you handled it according to Psalms 66:6.

TAKE YOUR NOTES

Position Your Faith for Great Success Workbook

Stephanie Franklin

Write down what you have received from the chapter and how it applies to your own life. How has your eyes been open? What areas will you change? What area(s) of success in your life will this benefit? Share your story by writing it below.

Stephanie Franklin

Position Your Faith for Great Success Workbook

Stephanie Franklin

Position Your Faith for Great Success Workbook

Stephanie Franklin

FAITH SESSION 3

Turn Your Water into Wine

There are times when God will tell you to do something that seem impossible or doesn't make sense. God loves to do the impossible in our lives because then it proves that there is no one and nothing greater than Him. He does this in order to get the glory and to increase your faith. Turn Your Water into Wine is based on God doing something that seems impossible in your life. I shared the story about Jesus turning water into wine. That is a miracle within itself. You can make the same miracle in your life, career, on your job, with your family, marriage, or children and turn it around from a defeated situation into a wining, victorious, and promotional success story. Turn your water into wine.

Answer the following questions from the book.

FAITH SESSION 3—Questions from the book.

Questions	DAY BY DAY GRACE CONFESSION OF FAITH
What was the container that Jesus filled? What was poured into the container? And how high was it filled?	
Why did the servants fill the containers?	I will better my career by
True or false. What page is it found on? "In this thing called **PURPOSE**, you may have to be alone."	

Position Your Faith for Great Success Workbook

What does turn your water into wine mean? _____ _____	**DAY BY DAY GRACE CONFESSION OF FAITH** I will better my career by _____ _____ _____ _____ _____ _____ _____ _____
True or false? God will never tell you to do something that you cannot do. _____ _____	
What have you gotten out of this chapter? _____ _____ _____	

> **Take the information from the session and discuss them in a group. Group discussion: Share your testimony of how you had to use your faith of obedience and obey God when He told you to do something that you did not understand, or could not see how it was going to turn out.**

Stephanie Franklin

TAKE YOUR NOTES

Stephanie Franklin

Write down what you have received from the chapter and how it applies to your own life. How has your eyes been open? What areas will you change? What area(s) of success in your life will this benefit? Share your story by writing it below.

Stephanie Franklin

Stephanie Franklin

Position Your Faith for Great Success Workbook

Stephanie Franklin

FAITH SESSION 3

When the Devil Steals Your Word of Faith

Have you ever listened attentively to someone speak some important, encouraging words of faith and later when you were alone and away from that or those persons you forgot what they said? Well, that's what I mean when I say the devil comes to steal your word of faith. It is not God's will that you forget vital and important information that will ultimately change your life for the better. This can hinder your success when this happens. You must pray and seek God about forgetfulness. If you are pressing towards great success, you must be able to obtain important information that is given to you. The devil comes to steal, kill, and to destroy. But Jesus comes that we may have life and have it more abundantly. *(John 10:10)*

Answer the following questions from the book.

FAITH SESSION 3—Questions from the book.

True or false. The word of faith I heard was from a dream.	**DAY BY DAY GRACE CONFESSION OF FAITH**
True or false. I believe that if you want to be delivered, God will immediately deliver you, but you must have faith that He can do it.	I will choose to remember that success comes
True or false. God moves according to your faith. What page is this statement found on?	

"**BELIEVE FOR YOURSELF.** "What subject is this referring too?	DAY BY DAY GRACE CONFESSION OF FAITH
	I will choose to remember that success comes
In the chapter, do you have to have a desire to change? How and what will you change about yourself in order to have great success?	
Can a person get delivered by just praying at times? Look for the answer based on what you have read in the chapter, not in your own words.	

Take the information from the session and discuss them in a group. Group discussion: Share about a time in your life when someone told you some vital information or you heard a speaker and before that day was over, you forgot everything that they said. What did you do? How did you handle it? How did you feel? How do you plan to change?

Stephanie Franklin

TAKE YOUR NOTES

Stephanie Franklin

Stephanie Franklin

> **Write down what you have received from the chapter and how it applies to your own life. How has your eyes been open? What areas will you change? What area(s) of success in your life will this benefit? Share your story by writing it below.**

Stephanie Franklin

Stephanie Franklin

Stephanie Franklin

FAITH SESSION 3

When the Lord Calls Your Name Say, "Here I am."

This chapter is based on your will to surrender to the Lord. It's based on your YES—what ever God tells you to do, you're ready to do it. Your success, your future, your life, your dreams, your purpose is caught in your ability to say yes to what God wants for you and your future. Did you enjoy reading this chapter? _____ If you said yes, good. This means that you're ready to obey God and say yes to what ever He tells you to do.

Let's see how you did reading the chapter. I want to quiz you over what you have read. Remember, your success is based on your ability to listen, learn, and grasp what you have heard, seen, and you getting out there to experience it for yourself.

Answer the following questions from the book.

FAITH SESSION 3—Questions from the book.

Questions	DAY BY DAY GRACE CONFESSION OF FAITH
What is the first thing God calls you out of after He calls your name?	I am chosen to succeed because
In the chapter, Peter took his eyes off of what caused him to sink?	
Does God call all of us the same? Why or why not?	

Position Your Faith for Great Success Workbook

Who was considered as a reject? Have you ever been rejected in your life? How and why? How did you handle it?	**DAY BY DAY GRACE CONFESSION OF FAITH**
What is the second thing God calls you out of after He calls your name?	I am chosen to succeed because
What is the last thing God calls you out of after He calls your name?	

Take the information from the session and discuss them in a group. Group discussion: Share about a time in your life when God was calling you into your ministry, or new career change, or personal changes in your life. Did you tell Him yes at first? How did you react? What did you do?

Stephanie Franklin

TAKE YOUR NOTES

Stephanie Franklin

Position Your Faith for Great Success Workbook

Stephanie Franklin

Write down what you have received from the chapter and how it applies to your own life. How has your eyes been open? What areas will you change? What area(s) of success in your life will this benefit? Share your story by writing it below.

Stephanie Franklin

Stephanie Franklin

Stephanie Franklin

Stephanie Franklin

FAITH SESSION 4

Let's pray before you begin.

Lord grant _____ the ability and the knowledge to complete this workbook. I thank You that _____ has comprehended and understood what has been written thus far. I pray for the full manifestation of success in _____ life after completing and reading this workbook. I thank You that _____ has learned and will retain all of the information after reading and studying this workbook. In Jesus Name, Amen.

FAITH SESSION 4

You Shall Have What you Speak

As you follow after your dreams and visions be careful what you speak. You can hinder the channel of blessings that is waiting for you. I'm not saying that your blessings will stop and not ever come to pass—as long as you are trusting in God, applying the word, and getting out there and putting in the work, you will still receive your blessings.

Let's see what this chapter has to say about watching what you speak. I want to quiz you over what you have read. I must say if you have gotten almost all of the answers right in this workbook, I am proud of you. You've done an excellent job! Pat yourself on the back. Now make room for me to pat you on the back……Great Job. Keep on going, you still have a ways to go to complete the workbook so keep reading and studying the book.

Answer the following questions from the book.

FAITH SESSION 4—Questions from the book.

Questions	DAY BY DAY GRACE CONFESSION OF FAITH
What is God <u>pleased with</u> in the beginning of this chapter?	I will watch what I speak because
What is God <u>not pleased</u> with in the beginning of the chapter?	
On page 362 what do you need to do if you have spoken words that are not pleasing to God?	

Position Your Faith for Great Success Workbook

What will happen when you love and speak highly of others, bless others, and speak words to will bring people to Christ?	**DAY BY DAY GRACE CONFESSION OF FAITH**
What has God reminded us?	I will watch what I speak because
Is this true? You should pick your friends wisely.	

Take the information from the session and discuss them in a group. Group discussion: Share about a time in your life when God was calling you into your ministry, or a new career change, or personal changes in your life. Did you tell Him yes at first? How did you react? What did you do?

TAKE YOUR NOTES

Stephanie Franklin

Stephanie Franklin

> **Write down what you have received from the chapter and how it applies to your own life. How has your eyes been open? What areas will you change? What area(s) of success in your life will this benefit? Share your story by writing it below.**

Position Your Faith for Great Success Workbook

Stephanie Franklin

Stephanie Franklin

Stephanie Franklin

FAITH SESSION 4

The Foundation is Already Laid

This **is your season of opportunity!** You have the power to do what has never been done before. You are on your way to your blessed, promised future! When you start thinking in terms of PURPOSE, you are moving towards your future, which is the promise that God has made to you.

Let's see how excited you were about reading this chapter. I have to admit that this is the most up tempo, upbeat, and encouraging chapter of the book. This chapter immediately sets you in a spirit of faith. It literally pushes you to believe through the word of God that this is your season and you can receive it—Just believe, obey, and receive! Let me quiz you, I know you're going to do well.

Answer the following questions from the book.

FAITH SESSION 4—Questions from the book.

Questions	DAY BY DAY GRACE CONFESSION OF FAITH
What happens when you start to think in terms of PURPOSE? 	This is my season of opportunity because
The foundation is already laid for you, how do you receive it? 	
What can move a mountain out of your way in your life that will keep you from succeeding? 	

Position Your Faith for Great Success Workbook

True or false. He wants you to experience the more than enough life.	**DAY BY DAY GRACE CONFESSION OF FAITH**
_____ _____ _____	
What was the only thing Adam and Eve had to do in order to receive their blessings? What page is this located on?	This is my season of opportunity because
_____ _____ _____	_____ _____ _____
True or false. God is way ahead of us all and He knows the plans that He has for you already and they are an expected end, not a dead end. What page is this located on?	_____ _____
_____ _____ _____	_____ _____ _____

Take the information from the session and discuss them in a group. Group discussion: Share with others, after reading this chapter in the book, how it has helped you. Also share what you have written in your workbook. Come together and compare answers and talk about them in your discussion.

Stephanie Franklin

TAKE YOUR NOTES

Stephanie Franklin

Write down what you have received from the chapter and how it applies to your own life. How has your eyes been open? What areas will you change? What area(s) of success in your life will this benefit? Share your story by writing it below.

Stephanie Franklin

Stephanie Franklin

FAITH SESSION 4

It's Your Appointed Season

This is your appointed season and don't allow anyone to tell you different! God has great things in-store for you. Many people said that you wouldn't make it. But you did. This is why you cannot give up! I believe if you have the faith and do not wait on others, God is about to move you into position and put you in a place to receive your harvest that is promised to you. Share your testimony when He does it and make sure you give Him all of the glory. The key here is that it's all in your faith. If you do not believe it will happen, it will not happen. But if you do believe, and go after it while at the same time trusting in God, you'll reap everything. I have heard success stories already!

Let's see how you've done in reading this powerful chapter.

Answer the following questions from the book.

FAITH SESSION 4—Questions from the book.

Questions	DAY BY DAY GRACE CONFESSION OF FAITH
What does the word, "Appointed" mean? What page is this located on?	
What does the word, "Season" mean? What page is this located on?	I will walk into my appointed season
What should you stay close too in order to receive your purpose and promise?	

What is a prayer partner of faith? What do you do with this or these persons? Is this someone you need to be with? _____ _____	**DAY BY DAY GRACE CONFESSION OF FAITH** I will walk into my appointed season _____ _____ _____ _____ _____ _____ _____
What was the out come of Jehoshaphat's story as it's used in the chapter? How does this apply to your own life? _____ _____ _____	
True or false. God said that this is your appointed season and no matter what battles are up against you, no matter how many giants are up against you, God's word will prevail. _____ _____ _____	

Take the information from the session and discuss them in a group. Group discussion: Share with others, after reading this chapter in the book how it has helped you. Also share what you have written in your workbook. Come together and compare answers and talk about them in your discussion.

Stephanie Franklin

TAKE YOUR NOTES

Stephanie Franklin

Stephanie Franklin

> **Write down what you have received from the chapter and how it applies to your own life. How has your eyes been open? What areas will you change? What area(s) of success in your life will this benefit? Share your story by writing it below.**

Stephanie Franklin

Stephanie Franklin

Position Your Faith for Great Success Workbook

Stephanie Franklin

FAITH SESSION 4

Stay Close to the Vine

It is so important to stay close to the vine. The vine is what will make you successful. The vine is what will make all of your dreams come true. Your career means nothing without the vine. No matter how hard life gets and no matter what hardships that may come your way, you must stay close to the vine. Remember the last two chapters that you just read and studied? "The Foundation is Already Laid' and "It's Your Appointed Season"? Well, all of your blessings in those chapters will come but you must stay close to the vine.

Let's see how you've done in reading yet another powerful chapter.

Answer the following questions from the book.

FAITH SESSION 4—Questions from the book.

Questions	DAY BY DAY GRACE CONFESSION OF FAITH
Who is the true vine? What page is this located on?	The vine in my life is _____
Why is it important to stay close to the vine?	
While it is your season, what can you not do? What page is this located on?	

Position Your Faith for Great Success Workbook

True or false. You must listen to God and He will tell you what your purpose and destiny is. He will always guide you up and not down.	**DAY BY DAY GRACE CONFESSION OF FAITH**
No faith, no purpose. No purpose, no story. No story, no God's glory. How does this apply to your life?	The vine in my life is
We have to stay looking up, keeping an open ear, obeying every word of the Lord, and climbing up our ladders of faith, purpose, and destiny. What happens when you do this?	

Take the information from the session and discuss them in a group. Group discussion: Share with others what the true vine means to you and how does the true vine apply to your life. Have you ever had to trust in the true vine? When? Where? Under what circumstances?

Stephanie Franklin

TAKE YOUR NOTES

Stephanie Franklin

Position Your Faith for Great Success Workbook

Write down what you have received from the chapter and how it applies to your own life. How has your eyes been open? What areas will you change? What area(s) of success in your life will this benefit? Share your story by writing it below.

Stephanie Franklin

Position Your Faith for Great Success Workbook

Stephanie Franklin

Position Your Faith for Great Success Workbook

7-DAY SERIES OF STUDY & FAST

Let's pray before you begin.

Lord grant _____ the ability and the knowledge to complete this 7-Day Series of Study. I thank You that _____ has comprehended and understood what has been written thus far in this workbook. I pray for the full manifestation of success in _____'s life after completing, studying, and fasting from this 7-Day Series of Study. I thank You that _____ has learned and will retain all of the information. In Jesus Name, Amen.

7-DAY SERIES OF STUDY & FAST
Position Your Faith for Great Success

How to understand fasting and the ability to see quick manifestations in your life:

In years past I have fasted only because pastor's or leader's have called a fast and as I attempted to follow their requests for each particular fast, I quickly realized that I was without full understanding of how to fast and how to see full blessings come into my life. As I matured in the Lord, gained deeper insight, and in my ministry, God has given me full understanding of how to fast according to the word of God and how to pray in order to bring quick manifestations in my life; and to remove the residue of doubt, unbelief, slothfulness, and lack of full knowledge and understanding. I felt led to add this 7—day series of study on fasting in my book because there are many people out there wondering why their prayers are not being answered after going on rigorous fasts or after being in constant prayer. I have the answers below for you. If you do not know how to fast or are uncertain about fasting, after applying and following this series, you will gain full knowledge and biblical insight and blessing by seeing full manifestations come from your fast as your prayers are quickly answered. Remember, in order for God to move in your life according to what you are praying and fasting for, **YOU MUST BELIEVE AND IGNITE YOUR FAITH. It will not work through doubting or unbelief.**

As I have been fasting the right way, I have notice quick returns on my fast and in my prayers. As quick as I started a fast, committed to what I chose to sacrifice for that period of time (food, etc.), applied the word of God daily, verbally confessed what I wanted and needed God to do in my life, God quickly answered my prayers in less than a day. I received quick breakthroughs almost immediately. But there have also been times when I did not do what I needed to do according to what a particular fast required, and noticed that my prayers were not answered right away—some were never answered and I gave up. This is not the will of God for His people. God desires to bless us. He desires that what ever we <u>sacrifice</u> for Him, will come to past according to His will. You cannot fast anything and expect it to come to past if it's not God's will and if it's not found in His word. Many people get this twisted. They believe that God should move no matter how they fast, how they pray, or what they are believing Him for. They say, "If He loves me, He should move." Or, "If God is real and He knows the desires of my heart, He should answer my prayers no matter what." These statements are true to a certain degree. They are true to the aspect that He does love you and He does desire to move for you, but He waits to <u>see</u> your <u>faith</u>. He waits to <u>see</u> your <u>sacrifice</u>. He waits to <u>see</u> if you're going to keep your <u>word</u>. He waits for you to apply

Position Your Faith for Great Success Workbook

His word and believe Him for what ever you're fasting and praying for. Make sense? I sure hope so.

Here is a* Step by Step Chart *to follow as you begin, during, and as you complete you're fast:

> **FASTING CHART:**
>
> 1. Decide what you want to sacrifice during your fast *(food, etc.)*.
> 2. Write down what you're fasting for *(healing, deliverance, peace, a financial breakthrough, spiritual blessings, family, etc.)*.
> 3. Find Scriptures in the bible that is only focused on what you are fasting for. *(If not familiar with the bible, use the concordance in the bible.)*
> 4. Write down your confession of faith *(what you are confessing in your life and/or others, what you are confessing out of your life.)*
> 5. Say and apply these steps *daily (during your fast)* and watch God move.

Here are some scriptures below that will give you biblical knowledge on fasting and the importance of fasting:

Mat 17:21	Howbeit this kind goeth not out but by prayer and fasting.
Mar 9:29	And he said unto them, This kind can come forth by nothing, but by prayer and fasting.
Psa 35:13	But as for me, when they were sick, my clothing [was] sackcloth: I humbled my soul with fasting; and my prayer returned into mine own bosom.
Dan 9:3	And I set my face unto the Lord God, to seek by prayer and supplications, with fasting, and sackcloth, and ashes:
1Cr 7:5	Defraud ye not one the other, except [it be] with consent for a time, that ye may give yourselves to fasting and prayer; and come together again, that Satan tempt you not for your incontinency.

I have provided a fast for the 7—Day Series of Study. You <u>may</u> do this fast. Follow the step by step chart above and watch God move in your life. Remember, in order for God to move in your life according to what you are praying and fasting for, **YOU MUST BELIEVE AND IGNITE YOUR FAITH. It will not work through doubting or unbelief.**
HERE WE GO. I KNOW YOU WILL DO WELL! >>>>>>>>>>>>>>>>>>>>>>>>>>>>>

Fast for healing, deliverance, and for great success. You may apply your own scriptures according to your need. I would give them to you but I do not know your need. The scriptures must be based upon your physical, spiritual, and/or mental need for you and/or for others.

God has promised, *"Is not the fast that I have chosen...[that] your healing shall spring forth speedily" (Isaiah 58:6,8)* When you begin fasting and praying for physical health and healing, you must realize that it is God that heals. His name is Jehovah Rapha means, *"I am the Lord who heals you" (Exodus 15:26)*

Name of Study:
Today's Date:
Your Focusing Scriptures:

7-DAY FAST 6AM-6PM

Eat only fruits and drink only water. You may eat soup, but no meats, punch, or soda after 6pm. You will study and stand on the scriptures below by reading and confessing them daily. You should do this even after you have finished the fast. Also follow the step by step chart above.

DAY	6am	12 noon	3pm	6pm
MONDAY				
TUESDAY				
WEDNESDAY				
THURSDAY				
FRIDAY				
SATURDAY				
SUNDAY				

Position Your Faith for Great Success Workbook

PREPARATION & CONFESSION FOR THE 7—SERIES OF STUDY FAST

PREPARATION & CONFESSION FOR THE 7—SERIES OF STUDY FAST

Aim: This fast is for healing, deliverance, and for great success. Specifically, I am fasting to _____
_____
_____

Confession: I believe God has healed, delivered, and has already given me great success in my life based on the scripture in Philippians 4:13 that, "I can do all things through Christ which strengthens me", and according to Isaiah 53:5 that says that by the strips of Jesus I am healed", and according to Nahum 1:9, that _____
_____ does not return back to me a second time. I believe that You Lord have great success for my life and I choose to follow that path that You have already prepared for me. I openly confess and commit my myself to Your healing, deliverance, and great success and will fast and pray for it until I see complete manifestations in my life and in the lives of others.

Bible Vision: "Is this not the fast I have chosen…your healing shall spring forth speedily" *(Isaiah 58:6, 8)*

Bible Promise: "The prayer of faith will save the sick, and the Lord will raise him up" *(James 5:15)*

Fast: What I will withhold/sacrifice _____

Beginning Date: _____
Ending Date: _____
Additional Resources: _____
_____
_____

Signed: _____
Date: _____

EXTRA NOTE PAD FOR 7-DAY FAST

If you are wondering what to take notes about you can write about how you're doing on your fast, did you fully complete the fast for the day, what your goals are for that particular day, etc.

EXTRA NOTE PAD FOR 7-DAY FAST

EXTRA NOTE PAD FOR 7-DAY FAST

EXTRA NOTE PAD FOR 7-DAY FAST

DAILY MORNING & EVENING BIBLE READING

Let's pray before you begin.

Lord grant _____ the ability and the knowledge to rise up every morning and before laying down at night the power to complete this morning and evening bible reading. I thank You that _____ has comprehended and understood what has been written thus far in this workbook. I pray for the full manifestation of success in _____ life after completing, studying, writing, and reading from this morning and evening bible reading. I thank You that _____ has learned and will retain all of the information. In Jesus Name, Amen.

Stephanie Franklin

DAILY MORNING & EVENING BIBLE READING

MONDAY

THEME SCRIPTURE FOR THE DAY
PURPOSE

Ecclesiastes 3:17

MORNING BIBLE READING on Joshua 3:10
Write your thoughts, notes, and day confession

EVENING BIBLE READING on Deuteronomy 31:6-8
Write your thoughts, notes, and night confession

Stephanie Franklin

TUESDAY

THEME SCRIPTURE FOR THE DAY
PURPOSE

Genesis 37:5, 39:2, 41: 41-45

Position Your Faith for Great Success Workbook

MORNING BIBLE READING on Acts 2:39
Write your thoughts, notes, and day confession

EVENING BIBLE READING on Romans 4:20
Write your thoughts, notes, and night confession

WEDNESDAY

THEME SCRIPTURE FOR THE DAY
PURPOSE

Romans 8:28

Position Your Faith for Great Success Workbook

MORNING BIBLE READING on Romans 4:17
Write your thoughts, notes, and day confession

EVENING BIBLE READING on Jeremiah 1:12
Write your thoughts, notes, and night confession

THURSDAY

THEME SCRIPTURE FOR THE DAY
PROMISE

Romans 4:21

Position Your Faith for Great Success Workbook

MORNING BIBLE READING on Jeremiah 32:17
Write your thoughts, notes, and night confession

EVENING BIBLE READING on Hebrews 11:6
Write your thoughts, notes, and night confession

Stephanie Franklin

FRIDAY

THEME SCRIPTURE FOR THE DAY
FOCUS

2 Timothy 1:7

Position Your Faith for Great Success Workbook

MORNING BIBLE READING on Galatians 6:9
Write your thoughts, notes, and night confession

EVENING BIBLE READING on 1 Thessalonians 5:17
Write your thoughts, notes, and night confession

SATURDAY

THEME SCRIPTURE FOR THE DAY
CHOSEN

Matthew 20:16

Position Your Faith for Great Success Workbook

MORNING BIBLE READING on Ephesians 1:4
Write your thoughts, notes, and night confession

EVENING BIBLE READING on John 15:16
Write your thoughts, notes, and night confession

SUNDAY

THEME SCRIPTURE FOR THE DAY
SUCCESS

Joshua 1:8

Position Your Faith for Great Success Workbook

MORNING BIBLE READING on Isaiah 48:15
Write your thoughts, notes, and night confession

EVENING BIBLE READING on Zachariah 8:12
Write your thoughts, notes, and night confession

END OF THE WEEK PRAYER

Father in the Name of Jesus, I thank You for dying on the cross just for my sins and for giving me the ability to see that I could not have made it through this week on my own. I give my purpose and success to You. It belongs to You anyway. I thank You that Your will shall be done and that I will have much success, prosperity, peace, happiness, joy, and protection without sorrow as I start another week standing on Your word, promises, and faith.

I can in no way complete my mission without You and I know that You will carry me through without fail according to Your word that says in *(Philippians 4:13) that "I can do all things through Christ which strengthens me."* In Jesus Name, amen.

QUESTIONS & ANSWERS OF SUCCESS

> **Let's pray before you begin.**
>
> Lord grant _____ the ability and the knowledge to complete this short series of questions and answers of success. I thank You that _____ has the motivation and the know how to get out there and to gain success. Thank You for granting favor and open doors. I pray for the full manifestation of success in _____'s life after completing these questions and answers of success. I thank You that _____ has learned and will retain all of the information. In Jesus Name, amen.

Stephanie Franklin

 QUESTIONS & ANSWERS OF SUCCESS
MAKE YOUR OWN ON THE NEXT PAGE

What defines great success?

Success is defined by the will to not give up, to leave past issues behind and start a new future, and to keep a clear mind; and to stay focused on career goals.

Where do you start if you want to be successful?

1. Know Who is your source—God. He provides everything and everyone you need. He is your visionary.
2. Use the vision that He has given to you. Don't be the servant in the bible who buried his talents, use what you have, get out there and show God that you have mustard seed faith so that God won't take your talents away and will give you more. *[The parable of the ten talents]*
3. When the going gets tough, you don't quit.
4. Create new avenues to win!
5. Encourage yourself by talking to yourself. Say, "_____ is going to win today." *(Add your name below)*
6. Always dream big and know that no dream is too big to accomplish.

EXTRA SPACE FOR YOU BELOW

_____
_____
_____
_____
_____
_____
_____
_____

Position Your Faith for Great Success Workbook

 # QUESTIONS & ANSWERS OF SUCCESS
ANSWER YOUR OWN ON THIS PAGE

What defines great success in my life?

_____
_____
_____

Where do I start if I want to be successful?

1.
2.
3.
4.
5.
6.

How do I define great success in my life?

_____
_____
_____

6 things in my life that defines great success:

(List them below)

1.
2.
3.
4.
5.
6.

BIBLE QUIZZES

Let's pray before you begin.

Lord grant _____ the ability and the knowledge to complete the bible quizzes. I thank You that _____ has comprehended and understood what has been written thus far in this workbook. I pray for the full manifestation of success in _____'s life after completing, writing, and studying, from these bible quizzes. I thank you that _____ has learned and will retain all of the information. In Jesus Name, Amen.

Stephanie Franklin

LET'S TEST YOUR BIBLE SKILLS

Some of the questions in this bible quiz may be somewhat challenging but do not give up, dig in the bible and push your faith, you can conquer this. I believe in you and I know you'll do fine. Let's go!

I. Titles & Names

Read the following questions, add the name of the person or person's that is listed to the right on the proper blank below.

1. The man that took the Israelites over the Red Sea? _____

2. He defeated the Giant Goliath in battle. _____

3. Which bird did Noah send out first from the ark? _____

4. These three were put in the fiery furnace. _____

5. What was the name of Jesus' mother?

NAMES:

Shadrach
David
Abednego
Raven
Moses
Mary
Meshach
Sarah
Mocking Bird
Hawk
Susan

MORE CHALLENGING QUESTIONS

The questions below are more challenging but do not give up, dig in the bible and push your faith, you can conquer this. I believe in you and I know you'll do fine. Let's go!

II. Titles

Read the following questions, add the name of the person or person's that is listed to the right on the proper blank below.

6. Considered as "The Giant Killer"
   _____

7. Considered as "The Lion Tamer"
   _____

8. Considered as "The Strong Man"
   _____

9. Considered as "The Wise King"
   _____

10. Considered as "Mr. Patience"
    _____

11. Considered as "The Man the was Crucified"
    _____

NAMES:

Jonah
Daniel
Job
David
Jesus
Solomon
Samson
Moses
Joseph
Cain
Abraham
Samuel
Paul

Stephanie Franklin

LET'S TEST YOUR BIBLE SKILLS

Can you put a name to each scripture? This may be challenging but do not give up! You're on your way to learning and understanding the bible better.

III. Who Said…….

Read the following questions, add the name of the Person or person's that is listed to the right on the proper blank below.

NAMES:

Jesus
Paul
Moses
Job
Hannah
Daniel
Ezekiel
Joseph
Mary

12. "For the wages of sin is death…"
    _____

13. "No prophet is accepted in his own country."
    _____

14. "The Lord gave and the Lord taketh away; blessed be the name of the Lord."
    _____

15. "Who is on the Lord's side? Let him come to me."
    _____

16. There is none holy as the Lord: for there is none beside thee: neither is there any rock like our God."
    _____

Position Your Faith for Great Success Workbook

LET'S TEST YOUR BIBLE SKILLS

Match up the spouses. They are all from the Old Testament.

IV. Match up the Spouses

Draw a line from the name on the left side to the name on the right side that matches.

17.	Abraham		Ruth
18.	Nahor		Sarah
19.	Jacob		Rachel
20.	Heber		Milcah
21.	Boaz		Jael

Stephanie Franklin

LET'S TEST YOUR BIBLE SKILLS

Multiple Choice, Old Testament.

V. Multiple Choice

Circle the answer that best fits the question.

22. Who were Shem, Ham, and Japheth?

    A. the wise men
    B. sons of Noah
    C. sons of Adam
    D. kings of Judah

23. David escaped from Achish the king of Gath by—

    A. disguising himself as a woman
    B. riding away on an ass at night
    C. feigning madness
    D. asking the Lord to make Achish blind and deaf

LET'S TEST YOUR BIBLE SKILLS

Multiple Choice, Old Testament.

V. Multiple Choice *con't.*

Circle the answer that best fits the question.

24. The Lord answered Job—

    A. "in a foreign tongue"
    B. "out of the whirlwind"
    C. "with a fierce anger"
    D. "in a tone he had not before heard"

25. The Book of Lamentations was written by—

    A. Ezekiel
    B. Jeremiah
    C. Amos
    D. Obadiah

LET'S TEST YOUR BIBLE SKILLS

VII. **Finish the faith scriptures below by looking in that particular chapter:**

26. **In 1 Chronicles chapter 17**
    O Lord. There is none like thee, _____ is _____ any God _____ thee, _____ to _____ that we have _____ with our _____.

27. **1 Chronicles chapter 17**
    Therefore now, Lord, let the thing that thou hast _____ concerning thy _____ and concerning his _____ be _____ for ever, and _____ as thou has said.

28. **Romans chapter 4**
    _____
    _____
    _____ calleth those things which be not as though they were.

LET'S TEST YOUR BIBLE SKILLS

VIII. True or false:

29. Delilah cut Samson's hair. True or False? _____
30. Before being cast into the sea, Jonah begged for time to say his prayers. True or False? _____
31. God performed a miracle similar to the parting of the Red Sea at the Jordan River. True or False? _____
32. The sound of the trumpets and rams' horns immediately proceeded the tumbling of the wall of Jericho. True or False? _____
33. When Joshua was fighting in Canaan, the sun stood still in the sky for forty days and for forty nights. True or False? _____
34. Solomon's temple was so grand that it was described as being larger by far than Noah's ark. True or False? _____
35. Elijah went to heaven on the back of a golden mule. True or False? _____
36. Job died shortly after his trials and tribulations. True or False? _____
37. Darius, ruler of Babylon, had Daniel thrown into the lion's den because he represented Daniel's praying to God. True or False? _____

ADD YOUR OWN CONFESSION OF FAITH TO WHAT GOD HAS PROMISED YOU WITH THESE SCRIPTURES

1 CHRONICLES 17: 23, 25-27

ROMANS 4: 13-22

ROMANS 5: 2-4

ROMANS 10:17

Stephanie Franklin

TAKE YOUR NOTES

Stephanie Franklin

DAILY PROMISES

Let's pray before you begin.

Lord grant _____ the ability and the knowledge to read and retain what has been read through the daily promises. I thank You that _____ has knows who he/she is and is confident that what you have promised, you will bring it to past. I pray for the full manifestation of success in _____'s life after reading and believing what each daily promise says. I thank you that _____ has learned and will retain all of the information. In Jesus Name, Amen.

DAILY PROMISES

MONDAY:

I WILL HAVE GREAT SUCCESS TODAY & NOTHING WILL HINDER IT.

TUESDAY:

MY FUTURE IS BRIGHT. MY LADDER DAYS ARE GREATER THAN MY PAST.

WEDNESDAY:

I AM BLESSED IN MY GOING AND IN MY COMING. THEREFORE, I WILL NOT BE MOVED BY ANYTHING THAT COMES TO STOP MY BLESSINGS.

THURSDAY:

GOD PROTECTS ME FROM DANGER THEREFORE I WILL WALK IN TRUST AND IN CONFIDENCE.

FRIDAY:

I WILL NOT DWELL ON MY PAST, BUT I WILL FOCUS ON MY PROMISED FUTURE THAT LIES AHEAD.

SATURDAY:

I CAN DO ALL THINGS THROUGH CHRIST WHO GIVES ME THE STRENGTH TO SUCCESSFULLY COMPLETE THEM.

SUNDAY:

I AM MORE THAN A CONQUEROR THROUGH JESUS CHRIST.

NOTES ON DAILY PROMISES

Stephanie Franklin

KEY--ANSWERS TO QUESTIONS
FROM VARIOUS CHAPTERS IN THE WORKBOOK

FAITH SESSION 1—Questions from the book.

Birthing Your Purpose from Your Pain

QUESTION

What is the key subject in Chapter One? After you write your answer below, discuss it with someone or in a group.

ANSWER:

Birthing your purpose from the pain of your past.

QUESTION

Can you tell me where and what page can you find this sentence? "Your purpose is what you were sent to the earth to do...."

ANSWER:

Pg. 61. Your purpose is what you were sent to the earth to do.

QUESTION

What was the number one encouragement that I told you in this chapter?

ANSWER:

Pg. 59. PLEASE DO NOT GIVE UP!

QUESTION

Why were these scriptures used in this chapter? Isaiah 44:2, Jeremiah 1:5, and Jeremiah 29:11.

ANSWER:

Pg. 61. You may ask, "How do I know what my purpose is?" I will answer you by saying that your purpose is what God has created you to do before you were created in your mother's womb *[Isaiah 44:2], [Jeremiah 1:5], [Jeremiah 29:11]*.

QUESTION

How do you win a person to Christ?

ANSWER:

Pg. 62. You must come down to their level in order to win them to Christ.

FAITH SESSION 1—Questions from the book.

Hell Faith to Heaven Faith

QUESTION

What is meant by hell faith to heaven faith?

ANSWER:

Pg. 80. If you do not believe in God, you are an unbeliever and this is what gives you hell faith. But if you believe in God and believe that He has saved you by dying for your sins; and the fact that you could not in no way have saved yourself, this is heaven faith.

QUESTION

If you do not believe in God is this Hell Faith or Heaven Faith? Why? Provide page number to back your answer up.

ANSWER:

Pg. 80. If you do not believe in God, you are an unbeliever and this is what gives you hell faith.

QUESTION

What is meant by Hell Faith to Heaven Faith?

ANSWER:

Pg. 80. [Galatians 6:14] says, "God forbid that we should glory in anyone or anything…"

QUESTION

What am I talking about concerning this sentence? *"This is what the devil believes..."* Elaborate using the extra space provided.

ANSWER:

Pg. 81. This is what the devil believes and he tries to block the channel of faith to many of those that he can, and turn what is the truth into a lie.

QUESTION

Can God lie? Find the answer in the chapter.

ANSWER:

Pg. 82. He will in no way leave you stranded nor will God ever put you to shame in front of the enemy to laugh and to ridicule you and say all manner of evil to you and about you. God will keep His word, because He cannot lie nor can He reverse it, and that is a promise. *[Numbers 23:19-20]*

FAITH SESSION 1—Questions from the book.

Faith as Easy as Saying 1, 2, 3

QUESTION

What is the rod that God is talking about in this chapter?

ANSWER:

Pg. 95. Moses inquired of the Lord, and the Lord told Moses to lift up the rod, and stretch it over the water and divide the water; and immediately when Moses obeyed the Lord, the waters divided and they all went across as the waters were still parted. This is the rod/stick that Moses used to get the people of Israel across the Red Sea by God's commands.

QUESTION

Finish this sentence: "As quick as it takes us to say, 1, 2, 3,..."

ANSWER:

Pg. 95. As quick as it takes us to say, 1, 2, 3, is as quick as it takes the Lord to answer your petition.

QUESTION

Who is David having the fight with in this chapter? How does he defeat him?

ANSWER:

Pg. 98. Goliath. He defeats him by hitting him in the head with a rock from his sling.

QUESTION

What is meant by, "it will not fail"?

ANSWER:

Pg. 97. But you have to trust that what ever God gives you, **it will not fail**.

QUESTION

What is meant by, "crazy faith"?

ANSWER:

Pg. 97. I'm sure that everyone who heard and saw little David step up to fight what seemed like a huge GIANT of a man, thought that he was crazy. But sometimes you gotta' have **crazy faith**. He had crazy faith because that's how much he loved God and trusted that God would give him what ever he needed to defeat the enemy.

QUESTION

How does this chapter relate to your own life? Use the extra writing space below for addition space to answer.

ANSWER:

Provide your own personal answer from your own life.

FAITH SESSION 1—Questions from the book.

Prosperity Come to me Right Now!

QUESTION

What is meant by "Prosperity Come to me Right Now"?

ANSWER:

Pg. 115. ...that we can command money to come to us instantly and it be done.

QUESTION

What is this sentence talking about? "Please do not miss your time waiting on God to make the first move."

ANSWER:

Pg. 115. But what God was waiting for, was for me to get up and do it first. God has given us the power to do it ourselves through His strength, power, ability, talent and most of all, through His faith which is through the word of God. Please do not miss your time waiting on God to make the first move. God is waiting on you to make the first move so that He can show you what He does when you show faith. God is ready to bless you and change your life forever.

QUESTION

When God is ready to take you to the next level do you have a choice?

ANSWER:

Pg. 117. But I've learned that when God is ready to take you higher, you do not have a choice in how He does it and the way He does it. Just trust that He knows what He is doing and will not lead you astray.

QUESTION

Pg. 119. Do you believe this is your appointed year by this sentence from the book? "I believe this is the year and season for the saints to receive everything that God has promised." Elaborate on your answer.

ANSWER:
Provide your own personal answer.

QUESTION
What is this phrase talking about? "It's yours for the asking and the taking?"

ANSWER:
Pg. 119. It's yours for the asking—the asking through prayer, believing by faith that you can have it. It's yours for the taking—the taking through faith believing through God's word. Asking and taking by leaning, trusting, and standing on the word of God.

QUESTION
What is meant by this? "But in the end when his so called friends found out that it was all God who orchestrated the entire test…"

ANSWER:
Pg. 118. But in the end when his so called friends found out that it was all God who orchestrated the entire test, they had to come back and repent to Job for doubting and coming against him. You must watch your mouth at all times.

FAITH SESSION 1—Questions from the book.

Don't Panic, it's Only a Test

QUESTION
What is meant by, "You see my glory, but you don't know my story."?

ANSWER:
Pg. 131. "You see my glory, but you don't know my story." What that simply means is that, they may see the anointing that sits on you right now, but they don't know what it took for you to get it.

QUESTION

How are the words, "church hurt" being used in this chapter? Explain.

ANSWER:

Pg. 132. It hurt so bad when I was hurt in the church, formally called: "church hurt". This is something that I almost never got over.

QUESTION

Expound on this statement in the chapter: "If we never have any enemies, we will never be challenged; and therefore we would get comfortable, and never go higher; therefore we would never fulfill the purpose that God has for us to fulfill."

ANSWER:

Pg.132. Use your own answer based on the statement written in the chapter.

QUESTION

From this statement, "HE DID NOT PANIC, BECAUSE HE KNEW THAT IT WAS ONLY A TEST." Who are they talking about?

ANSWER:

Pg. 133. Noah

QUESTION

Name the scripture that this statement is talking about. "He does not do it through unbelief, but is fully persuaded that what ever He promised you, He is more than able to perform it.

ANSWER:

Pg. 135. *[Romans 4:20-21], God says, "…that He staggers not at the promise through unbelief; but was strong in faith, giving glory to God." [21] And "…being fully persuaded that, what He had promised, He was more than able also to perform."*

QUESTION

What was the covenant that God made with Abraham in this chapter? And what type of relationship did they have?

ANSWER:

Pg. 137. Abraham was God's friend and there was nothing that God could keep from him, and even to that matter, wanted to keep anything from him. *[Genesis 18:17] Amplified* Abraham had that much faith and favor with the Lord. God knew that He could trust him to do what ever he was supposed to do, which was to fulfill the purpose and covenant that God had made with him to become a great nation.

✳✳

FAITH SESSION 1—Questions from the book.

It's a Set Up

QUESTION

Can you tell me where this sentence is in this chapter? "Giving up cannot be in your vocabulary."

ANSWER:

Pg. 153. Honestly to say that it's a set up. This is the time for you to trust God with all that you have. Giving up cannot be in your vocabulary. You cannot give up, God is with you---it may not seem like it, but trust Him, He is.

QUESTION

How is Matthew 26:36-42 being used in this chapter? What are your thoughts on it?

ANSWER:

Pg. 153. He never said fulfilling your purpose was going to be easy at times. Ask Jesus, He will tell you how challenging it was to fulfill the purpose and will of God while He was here on the earth, but the good news is, is that He did not give up, he said in *[Matthew 26:36-42]* to the Father as he prayed in Gethsemane: "*…nevertheless not as I will, but as thou wilt.*" Jesus was going through—He was troubled, and afraid; and He knew his time was near to go through much suffering for our sins.

QUESTION

What is the revelation to this sentence? "…One of those adhesives I use is called: "Elmer's Glue-All". It is a Multi-PURPOSE GLUE…"

ANSWER:

Pg. 157. I thought I was finished with this chapter but God has given me another revelation so I better write it down. I like to use all sorts of adhesives at times when making crafty 3-D objects in my spare time. One of those adhesives I use is called: "Elmer's Glue-All". It is a Multi-PURPOSE GLUE. The story is, I was working on an assignment at the time and the assignment called for the need to use the Elmer's glue. As I was working on the computer and gathering some saved drawings, my eyes happened to glance over to the glue as my eye balls quickly fixed on the words, "PURPOSE GLUE, BONDS STRONG FOR ALL YOUR NEEDS."

QUESTION

Finish this sentence from the chapter, "Just as this type of glue is intended for the use of adhesively bonding something together…"

ANSWER:

Pg. 158. Just as this type of glue is intended for the use of adhesively bonding something together, this is what God is to your life—He sticks to you like glue in order for you to come into the knowledge of who He is; and He pushes you to accomplish what purpose He has called, anointed, and appointed you to accomplish.

QUESTION

True or False. God is strictly intended to supply everything you stand in need of according to the purpose in which He has already set for you to accomplish.

ANSWER:

Pg. 158. True. God is strictly intended to supply everything you stand in need of according to the purpose in which He has already set for you to accomplish.

QUESTION

How is Jeremiah 29:11 being used in the chapter? Please answer according to what is written in the chapter.

ANSWER:

Pg. 159. So no matter what you are going through, just know it's only a setup. God does not come to make you loose or to destroy you, He comes to bless you and to give you an expected end. *[Jeremiah 29:11]*

FAITH SESSION 2—Questions from the book.

Iron Sharpens Iron

QUESTION

Can you tell me what areas in your life does God want to clean out in this chapter?"

ANSWER:

Pg. 171. Do you have a friend or are you in a relationship where you love that or those persons dearly but you two/all fight all the time? Do you ever allow the devil to play with your emotions and make you feel as if no one loves you? You may be there right now. Do you ever feel as if you just don't want to be bothered, and your friend, or husband, or wife, or family member, want to come and pour all of their bad day and problems out on you? Are you a selfish person who wants your way all the time? Is it hard for you to say you're sorry or admit when you're wrong? Do you seek to control people? Are you jealous of others accomplishments and feel left out? Do you live a lifestyle that contradicts the word of God? These are the areas that God wants to sharpen and clean out.

QUESTION

I mentioned about the refiners fire. What am I talking about and what is your perspective over this subject?

ANSWER:
Pg. 172. God is always convicting us in areas that we need to change. Kind of like the refiners fire and the fullers soap. *[Malachi 3:2-3]* God is a refiner and a purifier. He comes to purify everything that needs to be made clean.

QUESTION
What is meant by the potter wheel as it's being used in this chapter?

ANSWER:
Pg. 172. This is also like the potters wheel—the potter and the clay. *[Jeremiah 18: 1-6]* Have you ever been in the fire or on God's Potter's Wheel? God is the Potter, and you be the clay.

QUESTION
How are these words being used in the chapter? "My mind…..my emotions……my attitude…." How does this briefly relate to your own life?

ANSWER:
Pg. 173. The level that I'm speaking of was a level of trusting God to change *my mind*—my way of thinking on how I saw things. *My emotions*—how I thought no one loved me and couldn't trust people because of past hurts and disappointments. *My attitude*—how I reacted and perceived things, moving without consulting God first.

QUESTION
Finish this sentence from the chapter… "They mimic your actions and how you talk….."

ANSWER:
Pg. 174. They mimic your actions and how you talk. They watch your every move. They try to find something bad about you and expose it to the world. But even in their evil ways, God still delivers and He lifts up a standard against them. *[Isaiah 59:19]*

Position Your Faith for Great Success Workbook

QUESTION

What is the answer to this question from the chapter? "How do I get clean?" How does this apply to your own life?

ANSWER:

Pg. 181. You get clean by first of all repenting of the sin that you are doing, ask God to forgive you, and then you ask God to take away that or those very things that you are struggling with as you surrender it to Him. Before you know it, you'll feel better and you will be set free from that or those things that had you bound.

✸✸

FAITH SESSION 2—Questions from the book.

Two Heads Are Better Than One

QUESTION

Why did I make this statement in the chapter? "One thing you have to realize is that you cannot complete your purpose by yourself."

ANSWER:

Pg. 194. One thing you have to realize is that you cannot complete your purpose by yourself. God places people in your life to be a help to get you where you need to be. He wants to fulfill His purpose in you and through you. When God has assigned certain people to come into your life, be careful that you do not block them out; they will play a very important key piece in your life.

QUESTION

"God will never put two people together and their destinies and plans do not match." What is the next sentence after this one? And what does this mean?

ANSWER:

Pg. 195. God will never put two people together and their destinies and plans do not match. He will always put you with someone who's going in the same direction you are.

QUESTION

Why does God want you to be happy? What is meant by this sentence? What page is it located on? Apply this to your life.

ANSWER:

Pg. 196. God wants you to be happy. He wants you to be married if you so desire. This is why He created Adam and Eve to be a help-mate for Adam. They both are together. They both are one. Two heads are better than one.

QUESTION

What happens when people jump into relationships too quick?

ANSWER:

Pg. 196. It just means that the person did not wait on God's instructions and they moved before God and allowed sin to come in and bring destruction. Now you two have to start all over again. This is why you two argue and fight all the time because you did not wait on God. Don't get in the flesh and do your own thing. This brings catastrophe, heartaches, torment, turmoil, and maybe even deadly outcomes.

QUESTION

On page 194, who's plans can you destroy before they manifest? What scripture is based from this?

ANSWER:

Pg. 194. *[1 Thessalonians 5:17]* You should pray in such away—everyday that when the devil tries to come with his tricks and schemes, you can destroy his plans before they can ever manifest.

QUESTION

"When God has assigned certain people to come into your life, be careful that you do not block them out..." Why is this important according to the chapter?

ANSWER:

Pg. 194. When God has assigned certain people to come into your life, be careful that you do not block them out; they will play a very important key piece in your life. Pushing them away will only set you back and delays your blessing that God has lined up for you.

FAITH SESSION 2—Questions from the book.

You Are Special Like the Cedar Tree

QUESTION
Why do people wear masks?

ANSWER:
Pg. 209. We wear masks only to hide the real truth that lies within each one of us for the fear of everybody knowing the truth.

QUESTION
What does Ezekiel 31:1-9 mean to you?

ANSWER:
Pg. 211. Answer question in your own words from this page.

QUESTION
What page is this statement on? "When you are chasing after purpose, you are not chasing after people." What does this mean to you?

ANSWER:
Pg. 214. Add your own opinion.

QUESTION

What happens when you chase after people?

ANSWER:

Pg. 214. When you chase after people, you will be led in the wrong direction. They will get you off focus, and you are worse off than you were before you made the mistake in allowing them to lead you in the first place

QUESTION

What happens when God begin to bless you according to page 217?

ANSWER:

Pg. 217. I want to give you some great news, that when God begins to bless you, no one will be able to hide God's greatness in you, they will not be able to hide the great anointing that's on your life, they will not be able to hide the great ministry that God is building in you, they will not be able to speak against what God is doing in your life and in your family.

QUESTION

How does this statement apply to your own life? "He healed you to a greater glory and a greater testimony." *Found on page 218*

ANSWER:

Use your own answer according to your own opinion.

QUESTION

Psalms 68:1 says according to this chapter. How is it being used?

ANSWER:

Pg. 217. Their jealousy will not be able to fester and cause all kinds of embarrassment. God will arise. He will arise in you and each one of your enemies will be scattered. The bible says, *"Let God arise, let his enemies be scattered...." [Psalms 68:1]* God will arise in your situation and in your life and all of your enemies will be scattered.

Position Your Faith for Great Success Workbook

FAITH SESSION 2—Questions from the book.

Don't Judge A Book by it's Cover

QUESTION

"Ever had someone to judge you from what they thought they saw on the outside?" What page is this located on, and how does this apply to you?

ANSWER:
Pg. 229. Add your own thoughts and story.

QUESTION

True or false. Does God want His people to have great success based on page 231-232.

ANSWER:
True. God wants His people to have great success. He wants your future to soar. He wants you to be on top and not at the bottom.

QUESTION

True or false. God will never give up on you. Explain your answer.

ANSWER:
Pg. 231. True

QUESTION

Why does God want your future to soar?

ANSWER:

Pg. 232. He wants your future to soar because, "You are victorious and that you are somebody, God is a forgiver of mistakes and sins, you are beautiful and not ugly, you do have a future…"

QUESTION

Do not be afraid of walking and living a life of success. What page is this statement on and how does it apply to your own life?

ANSWER:

Pg. 233. Add your own opinion based on your own life.

QUESTION

Take hold of your future! Reposition your faith for greatness for your future! Do you believe this statement? Why?

ANSWER:

Pg. 233. Add your own statement to this question.

***

FAITH SESSION 2—Questions from the book.

The Potter and the Clay

QUESTION

"…God is trying to make each and every one of us into something beautiful to look at—from the inside out." How does this apply to your own life?

ANSWER:

Pg. 247. Answer in your own words.

QUESTION

True or false. When you are representing God you are not required to be just like Him. Why or why not?

ANSWER:
Pg. 247. False. If you are going to represent Him, you have got to be just like Him.

QUESTION
Who is the Potter and who is the clay in the chapter?

ANSWER:
Pg. 247. Who is the Potter? The Potter is the Lord, and who is the piece of clay? The piece of clay is us human beings.

QUESTION
What is God trying to create in you, He as the Potter and you as the clay?

ANSWER:
Pg. 247. God is trying to make each and every one of us into something beautiful to look at—from the inside out.

QUESTION
Why do we fight God's purpose and plan for our lives?

ANSWER:
Pg. 248. We fight God's purpose and plan for our lives. We fight the fact that while God is changing, forming, and cleansing us, by the fact that it hurts and it's by the fact that it's uncomfortable.

QUESTION
In the first synopsis, what example is used and what is stated in the chart?

ANSWER:
Pg. 250-253. It shows an example of a stick figure person that you are to create and write out the person that God is creating you to be.

FAITH SESSION 2—Questions from the book.

I Am All That God Says I Am

QUESTION
What will make you soon forget that you are special like God says you are?

ANSWER:
Pg. 265. **"I am all that God says I am"** can be very challenging at times to believe especially when life's struggles, trials, and tribulations; and negative words of people come to make you forget.

QUESTION
True or false. Your future may seem very dim, but God will resurrect your future.

ANSWER:
Pg. 265. True. Your future may seem very dim, but God will resurrect your future.

QUESTION
Was Lazarus raised from the dead immediately?

ANSWER:
Pg. 266. Yes. *[verse 17]* Lazarus was raised from the dead immediately.

QUESTION
What page is this statement located on? "Your latter days shall be greater than your former days."

ANSWER:
Pg. 266. Located at the very bottom.

QUESTION

What page is this statement on? "But when Jesus came into the room, the defeated situation changed into a **resurrection experience** and Lazarus was raised from the dead.

ANSWER:

Pg. 266. Located in the middle of the page.

QUESTION

Is God doubting your situation?

ANSWER:

Pg. 268. God is not doubting your situation; He's already made plans to bring you out with the victory.

FAITH SESSION 3—Questions from the book.

Can These Dry Bones Resurrect and Live?

QUESTION

What is this chapter talking about? *(Must be the exact words from the chapter)*

ANSWER:

Pg. 281. It will show you how to make your dry bones live again. It will show you that God is your way out. He will make your dry bones come alive and live again.

QUESTION

"Your circumstances have out weighed what the word of God has told you about God being a promise keeper." What does it talk about next?

ANSWER:

Pg. 281. [Hebrews 6:13-18] God's promise—His oath is unchanging.

Stephanie Franklin

QUESTION

"Can your finances get any better than just making it from pay check to pay check?" What's the answer to this sentence in the chapter?

ANSWER:

Pg. 282. In verse 4 God says: *"prophesy and say, "O' you dry bones, hear the word of the Lord. Verse 5, thus says the Lord God to these bones: Behold, (take a look at, watch, observe) I will cause breath and spirit to enter you, and you shall live."* You have to take hold of your life and command your situation to change by speaking words of faith and using the word of the Lord.

QUESTION

"You've been... following the same ol' people that mean your future no good, you've been doubting yourself and allowing the same ol' people to dictate your life...." What is the Holy Spirit saying after this?

ANSWER:

Pg. 284. The Holy Spirit is telling you today that God is ready for you to go to another level.

QUESTION

True or false. You must rebuke the devil and his tactics to make you quit and abort the promise that God is leading you to, and command your future to be blessed.

ANSWER:

Pg. 282. True. You must rebuke the devil and his tactics to make you quit and abort the promise that God is leading you to, and command your future to be blessed.

QUESTION

True or false? You have to take hold of your life and command your situation to change by speaking words of faith and using the word of the Lord.

ANSWER:

Pg. 282. You have to take hold of your life and command your situation to change by speaking words of faith and using the word of the Lord. Speak to those dry, dead bones in your life and tell them to change, tell them to live, tell your blessings to come to you right now.

FAITH SESSION 3—Questions from the book.

When My Bones Became Flesh through Faith

QUESTION

What was explained in the chapter, "Can These Dry Bones Resurrect and Live?"

ANSWER:

Pg. 295. I explained in the chapter, "Can These Dry Bones Resurrect and Live?" that you have the power and the faith to change a dead situation that seems as if it is impossible to change. You have the power to move old, depressing, unimportant things out of your life by simply telling them to move.

QUESTION

True or false. You do not have the power to move old, depressing, unimportant things out of your life by simply telling them to move.

ANSWER:

Pg. 295. False. You <u>do</u> have the power to move old, depressing, unimportant things out of your life by simply telling them to move.

QUESTION

What page is this located on? What is it talking about? "You can get everything that has been stolen from you back."

ANSWER:

Pg. 296. But in this chapter it proves that your dry bones can come back alive and live. You can get everything that has been stolen from you back.

QUESTION

What page and what scripture is this statement being used as an example? "God can make you new."

ANSWER:

Pg. 297. *[2 Corinthians 5:17] "Old things are past away, behold all things have become new."* God can make you new.

QUESTION

"You have to literally tell yourself that you can make it and speak God's word…" What is this referring too? What page?

ANSWER:

Pg. 297. …I can recall a time when I did not have a job and had given up. Every job that I applied to or went to an interview, either I was under qualified, or I was over qualified. *(Sharing my testimony of having no job.)*

QUESTION

How does the statement apply to your own life?

ANSWER:

This answer requires a statement from the reader.

FAITH SESSION 3—Questions from the book.

Turn Your Water into Wine

QUESTION

What was the container that Jesus filled? What was poured into the container? And how high was it filled?

ANSWER:

Pg. 311. The bible says in verse 7 that Jesus told the servants, the ones that Mary instructed to listen to Jesus to fill the water pots with water. They filled the pots to the brim.

QUESTION

Why did the servants fill the containers?

ANSWER:

Pg. 312. The servants filled the water to the top because they knew that if Mary said to listen to Jesus, they were confident that everything was going to be alright; and they wanted to see how in the world was he going to turn that pot of water into wine.

QUESTION

True or false. What page is it found on? "In this thing called **PURPOSE**, you may have to be alone."

ANSWER:

Pg. 313. True. In this thing called **PURPOSE**, you may have to be alone.

QUESTION

What does turn your water into wine mean?

ANSWER:

Pg. 314. Turn your water into wine means you're going to have to trust God to do the impossible, reach the unreachable, do the unthinkable, and see what has never been seen before.

QUESTION

True or false? God will never tell you to do something that you cannot do.

ANSWER:

Pg. 314. God will never tell you to do something that you cannot do.

QUESTION
What have you gotten out of this chapter?

ANSWER:
Answer question in your own words.

***

FAITH SESSION 3—Questions from the book.

When the Devil Steals Your Word of Faith

QUESTION
True or false. The word of faith I heard was from a dream.

ANSWER:
Pg. 325. False. One day, years ago, I <u>was sitting and listening to a preacher preach his sermon.</u> Just as I was sitting and listening to his sermon and the words that he spoke, they quickly went in one ear, and out of the other.

QUESTION
True or false. I believe that if you want to be delivered, God will immediately deliver you, but you must have faith that He can do it.

ANSWER:
Pg. 326. True. I believe that if you want to be delivered, God will immediately deliver you, but you must have faith that He can do it.

QUESTION
True or false. God moves according to your faith. What page is this statement found on?

ANSWER:
Pg. 327. True. God does move according to your faith.

Position Your Faith for Great Success Workbook

QUESTION
"**BELIEVE FOR YOURSELF.** "What subject is this referring too?

ANSWER:
Pg. 327. You have to **BELIEVE FOR YOURSELF** that what they said to you is a true word from God.

QUESTION

In the chapter, do you have to have a desire to change? How and will you change about yourself in order to have great success?

ANSWER:
Answer question in your own words.

QUESTION

Can a person get delivered by just praying at times? Look for the answer based on what you have read in the chapter, not in your own words.

ANSWER:

Pg. 326. I believe that if you want to be delivered, God will immediately deliver you, but you must have faith that He can do it. Now don't get me wrong, sometimes deliverance is a process—it does not always happen over night. But I can rest assure you that if you hang in there, keep applying the word of God, confessing that you are delivered by speaking in your healing with your mouth; and fasting, you will find that your deliverance will happen almost before you realize it.

***

FAITH SESSION 3—Questions from the book.

When the Lord Calls Your Name Say, "Here I am."

QUESTION

What is the first thing God calls you out of after He calls your name?

ANSWER:
Pg. 331. He calls you out of your past.

QUESTION
In the chapter, Peter took his eyes off of what caused him to sink?

ANSWER:
Pg. 341. As soon as Peter took his eyes off of Jesus and the PURPOSE that Jesus had asked him to do, he began to sink; and to a point where he had to cry out for Jesus to help him. *[Matthew14:22-36]*

QUESTION
Does God call all of us the same? Why or why not?

ANSWER:
Pg. 342. God calls each one of us differently and at different times.

QUESTION
Who was considered as a reject? Have you ever been rejected in your life? How and why? How did you handle it?

ANSWER:
Pg. 242. Moses was rejected.

QUESTION
What is the second thing God calls you out of after He calls your name?

ANSWER:
Pg. 343. He calls you into the/your ministry.

QUESTION
What is the last thing God calls you out of after He calls your name?

ANSWER:
Pg. 348. He calls you into your purpose.

FAITH SESSION 4—Questions from the book.

You Shall Have What you Speak

QUESTION

What is God pleased with in the beginning of this chapter?

ANSWER:

Pg. 361. God is pleased when good, positive, and wholesome things come out of our mouths.

QUESTION

What is God not pleased with in the beginning of the chapter?

ANSWER:

Pg. 361. He is not pleased when we speak things that are contrary to His Word *(bible)*.

QUESTION

On page 362 what do you need to do if you have spoken words that are not pleasing to God?

ANSWER:

Pg. 362. All you have to do is confess your sin to God by repenting for allowing those words to come out of your mouth, ask Him to forgive you, and then ask Him to deliver you so that you will not speak in that way again.

QUESTION

What will happen when you love and speak highly of others, bless others, and speak words to will bring people to Christ?

ANSWER:

Pg. 362, I'm a strong believer when you love and speak highly of others, bless others, and speak words to will bring people to Christ, your days will be filled with the victory over every situation and you'll be blessed.

QUESTION

What has God reminded us?

ANSWER:

Pg. 362. God has reminded us that He is true to His promise and that He will not fail us.

QUESTION

Is this true? You should pick your friends wisely.

ANSWER:

Pg. 365. Yes, true. You should pick your friends wisely.

FAITH SESSION 4—Questions from the book.

The Foundation is Already Laid

QUESTION

What happens when you start to think in terms of PURPOSE?

ANSWER:

Pg. 379. When you start thinking in terms of PURPOSE, you are moving towards your future, which is the promise that God has made to you.

QUESTION

The foundation is already laid for you, how do you receive it?

ANSWER:

Pg. 379. The foundation is already laid for you to receive it. The key is, just receive it. Well, you may ask, "how do I go about receiving it?" Well the answer to that question is simple, **JUST RECEIVE IT**.

QUESTION

What can move a mountain out of your way in your life that will keep you from succeeding?

ANSWER:

Pg. 379. The bible says in *[Matthew 17:20]* that faith the size of a mustard seed can MOVE MOUNTAINS. Do you know how huge mountains are? Moving one would seem impossible. But the bible says with just a little grain of a mustard seed can move a huge mountain out of your way.

QUESTION

True or false. He wants you to experience the more than enough life.

ANSWER:

Pg. 380. True. He does want you to experience the more than enough life.

QUESTION

What was the only thing Adam and Eve had to do in order to receive their blessings? What page is this located on?

ANSWER:

Pg. 382. All Adam and Eve had to do was BELIEVE, OBEY, AND RECEIVE. All they had to do was to have faith that God had already laid the foundation by doing all of the hard work, and all they had to do was **receive the blessings that God had already laid before them**. All they had to do was REAP THE HARVEST.

QUESTION

True or false. God is way ahead of us all and He knows the plans that He has for you already and they are an expected end, not a dead end. What page is this located on?

ANSWER:
Pg. 386, True. God is way ahead of us all and He knows the plans that He has for you already and they are an expected end, not a dead end. *[Jeremiah 29:11]*

****

FAITH SESSION 4—Questions from the book.

It's Your Appointed Season

QUESTION
What does the word, "Appointed" mean? What page is this located on?

ANSWER:
Pg. 403. The word <u>Appointed</u> means: "chosen, selected, prearranged, to appoint".

QUESTION
What does the word, "Season" mean? What page is this located on?

ANSWER:
Pg. 403. The word <u>Season</u> means: "period, time, term, time of year".

QUESTION
What should you stay close too in order to receive your purpose and promise?

ANSWER:
Pg. 403. *You must stay close to the vine* in order to fulfill your purpose and receive the promise.

QUESTION
What is a prayer partner of faith? What do you do with this or these persons? Is this someone you need to be with?

ANSWER:

Pg. 405. A prayer partner of faith is someone who's going to talk, walk, and live positive even when they cannot visually see your breakthrough, or how it's going to workout for you. They trust God for you and with you until they see God move in your circumstances.

QUESTION

What was the out come of Jehoshaphat's story as it's used in the chapter? How does this apply to your own life?

ANSWER:

Pg. 406. The outcome of Jehoshaphat's trial was that he did all that God told him to do as the Lord GAVE INSTRUCTION. God gave specific instructions to Jehoshaphat and all of Judah through the prophet Jahaziel the son of Zechariah. The spirit of the Lord came upon him and said in *[verse 16-17]*, *"Be not afraid or dismayed at this great multitude; for the battle is not yours, but God's. [17] Ye shall not need to fight in this battle: set yourselves, stand still, and see the salvation of the Lord with you, O Judah and Jerusalem: fear not, nor be dismayed: tomorrow go out against them: for the Lord will be with you."*

QUESTION

True or false. God said that this is your appointed season and no matter what battles are up against you, no matter how many giants are up against you, God's word will prevail.

ANSWER:

Pg. 406. True. God said that this is your appointed season and no matter what battles are up against you, no matter how many giants are up against you, God's word will prevail.

FAITH SESSION 4—Questions from the book.

Stay Close to the Vine

QUESTION
Who is the true vine? What page is this located on?

ANSWER:
Pg. 421. The true vine is the Lord.

QUESTION
Why is it important to stay close to the vine?

ANSWER:
Pg. 421. If you break the vine, you break any contact you have with the Lord.

QUESTION
While it is your season, what can you not do? What page is this located on?

ANSWER:
Pg. 422. While it is your season you must stay close to the vine. You cannot waver nor can you doubt. You must keep your ears open to the voice of God, obey His voice, and move when He tells you to move.

QUESTION
True or false. You must listen to God and He will tell you what your purpose and destiny is. He will always guide you up and not down.

ANSWER:
Pg. 423. True. You must listen to God and He will tell you what your purpose and destiny is. He will always guide you up and not down.

QUESTION
No faith, no purpose. No purpose, no story. No story, no God's glory. How does this apply to your life?

ANSWER:
Pg. 423. Answer this question in your own words.

QUESTION

We have to stay looking up, keeping an open ear, obeying every word of the Lord, and climbing up our ladders of faith, purpose, and destiny. What happens when you do this?

ANSWER:

Pg. 423. We have to stay looking up, keeping an open ear, obeying every word of the Lord, and climbing up our ladders of faith, purpose, and destiny. When you do this, this is how you turn your faith towards your future. Now all you have to do is walk in it.

7-DAY SERIES OF STUDY & FAST

No answers needed

DAILY MORNING & EVENING BIBLE READING

No answers needed

QUESTIONS & ANWERS OF SUCCESS

No answers needed

BIBLE QUIZZES—ANSWERS

1. Moses, (Exodus 15:22)
2. David, (I Samuel 17:23)
3. Raven, (Genesis 8:7)
4. Shadrach, Meshach, Abednego, (Daniel 3:19-23)
5. Mary, (Matthew 1:18)
6. David, (I Samuel 17)

7. Daniel, (Daniel 6)
8. Samson, (Judges 14-16)
9. Solomon, (I Kings 3-11)
10. Job, (Job)
11. Jesus,
12. Paul, (Romans 6:23)
13. Jesus, (Luke 4:24)
14. Job, (Job 1:21)
15. Moses, (Exodus 32:26)
16. Hannah, (I Samuel 2:2)
17. Sarah, (Genesis 17:15)
18. Milcah, (Genesis 11:29)
19. Rachel, (Genesis 29:28)
20. Jael, (Judges 4:17)
21. Ruth, (Ruth 4:13)
22. B, (Genesis 5:32, 6:10)
23. C, (I Samuel 21:12-15)
24. B, (Job 38:1)
25. B, (Lamentations)
26. ANSWER WITHIN CHAPTER
27. ANSWER WITHIN CHAPTER
28. ANSWER WITHIN CHAPTER
29. False, (Judges 16:19)
30. False, (Jonah 1:12-15)
31. True, (Joshua 3:15-17)
32. False, (Joshua 6:20)
33. False, (Joshua 10:13)
34. False, (Genesis 6:15; 2 Chronicles 3:3)
35. False, 2 Kings 2:11)
36. False, (Job 42:16)
37. False, (Daniel 6:12-16)

DAILY PROMISES

No answers needed

About the Author

Stephanie's the best-selling author of, "When Ramona Got Her Groove Back from God". She is also the author of My Song of Solomon, My Song of Solomon *Prayer Journal,* and Position Your Faith for Great Success. Stephanie is letting her multi-talents shine, but within all of these talents she's quick to give God all the glory. She is an author, playwright, director, producer, poet, designer, illustrator, motivational speaker, minister, entrepreneur, and educator. Evangelist Stephanie Franklin is all of these things and more. She speaks to the hearts of those who are in need of a life transformation and an up-lifting spiritual and mental move. God has called, anointed, and appointed her to be a Prophetess and to evangelize the world. She is very humble in allowing God to use her spiritual gifts in prophecy, healing, and deliverance. As a result, many people have been uplifted, healed, and delivered under her powerful prophetic ministry.

Her novels have so many twists and turns that will keep you on the edge of your seat and your eyes flowing through every line. Her spiritual realism, dazzling—heart turning and soul moving novels will make you want to change your life at a heart beat. Her books of faith, success, and purpose will turn your faith and determination towards a whole new dimension of, if you just have faith and confidence in yourself, you can do the impossible. Her work ministers to the hearts of millions all over the world, inspiring them to change, and challenging them to love and to live a new and wholesome life.

www.ingramcontent.com/pod-product-compliance
Lightning Source LLC
Chambersburg PA
CBHW082143230426
43672CB00015B/2836